Makerspace and Collaborative Technologies

The Library of Object Relations

Marta Mestrovic Deyrup, Ph.D.
Acquisitions Editor, Library Information and Technology Association,
a division of the American Library Association

The Library Information Technology Association (LITA) Guides provide information and guidance on topics related to cutting-edge technology for library and IT specialists.

Written by top professionals in the field of technology, the guides are sought after by librarians wishing to learn a new skill or to become current in today's best practices.

Each book in the series has been overseen editorially since conception by LITA and reviewed by LITA members with special expertise in the specialty area of the book.

Established in 1966, LITA is the division of the American Library Association (ALA) that provides its members and the library and information science community as a whole with a forum for discussion, an environment for learning, and a program for actions on the design, development, and implementation of automated and technological systems in the library and information science field.

Approximately 25 LITA Guides were published by Neal-Schuman and ALA between 2007 and 2015. Rowman & Littlefield took over publication of the series beginning in late 2015. Books in the series published by Rowman & Littlefield are:

Digitizing Flat Media: Principles and Practices
The Librarian's Introduction to Programming Languages
Library Service Design: A LITA Guide to Holistic Assessment, Insight, and Improvement
Data Visualization: A Guide to Visual Storytelling for Librarians
Mobile Technologies in Libraries: A LITA Guide
Innovative LibGuides Applications
Integrating LibGuides into Library Websites
Protecting Patron Privacy: A LITA Guide
The LITA Leadership Guide: The Librarian as Entrepreneur, Leader, and Technologist
Using Social Media to Build Library Communities: A LITA Guide
Managing Library Technology: A LITA Guide
The LITA Guide to No- or Low-Cost Technology Tools for Libraries
Big Data Shocks: An Introduction to Big Data for Librarians and Information Professionals
The Savvy Academic Librarian's Guide to Technological Innovation: Moving Beyond the Wow Factor
The LITA Guide to Augmented Reality in Libraries
Digital Curation Projects Made Easy: A Step-By-Step Guide for Libraries, Archives, and Museums

Library Technology Planning for Today and Tomorrow: A LITA Guide
Tech for All: Moving beyond the Digital Divide
Change Management for Library Technologists: A LITA Guide
Makerspace and Collaborative Technologies: A LITA Guide

Makerspace and Collaborative Technologies

A LITA Guide

Edited by
Beth Thomsett-Scott

ROWMAN & LITTLEFIELD
Lanham • Boulder • New York • London

Published by Rowman & Littlefield
An imprint of The Rowman & Littlefield Publishing Group, Inc.
4501 Forbes Boulevard, Suite 200, Lanham, Maryland 20706
www.rowman.com

6 Tinworth Street, London SE11 5AL

Copyright © 2020 by American Library Association

All rights reserved. No part of this book may be reproduced in any form or by any electronic or mechanical means, including information storage and retrieval systems, without written permission from the publisher, except by a reviewer who may quote passages in a review.

British Library Cataloguing in Publication Information Available

Library of Congress Cataloging-in-Publication Data

Names: Thomsett-Scott, Beth C., editor.
Title: Makerspace and collaborative technologies : a LITA guide / edited by Beth Thomsett-Scott.
Description: Lanham : Rowman & Littlefield Publishing Group, [2020] | Series: LITA guides | Includes bibliographical references and index. | Summary: "This book explores how patrons are using innovative technologies utilizing real-life case studies from a variety of academic institutions. Discover which technologies patrons are using, how they are using them, and the purposes of use. Authors include best practices on designing space, marketing the technology, and collaborating to enhance the use"—Provided by publisher.
Identifiers: LCCN 2019041369 (print) | LCCN 2019041370 (ebook) | ISBN 9781538126479 (cloth) | ISBN 9781538126486 (paperback) | ISBN 9781538126493 (epub)
Subjects: LCSH: Academic libraries—Information technology—United States. | Academic libraries—Technological innovations—United States. | Makerspaces in libraries. | Academic libraries—United States—Case studies.
Classification: LCC Z675.U5 M3247 2020 (print) | LCC Z675.U5 (ebook) | DDC 027.7—dc23
LC record available at https://lccn.loc.gov/2019041369
LC ebook record available at https://lccn.loc.gov/2019041370

Contents

Figures ix

Introduction xi
   Paul McMonigle

1 Engaging Users with Technology at the University of Florida Libraries 1
   Samuel Putnam

2 John Peace Library and the Applied Engineering and Technology Library, University of Texas at San Antonio 13
   Matt Hayward

3 Lightboard and ArcGIS and Solstice, Oh My! 25
   Becca Greenstein

4 The Holographic Landscape: 3D Modeling for the HoloLens 37
   Dean Walton

5 Creating Ideas into Reality: Spaces and Programs That Open Up the Imagination 51
   Kari Kozak

6 Planning, Implementing, and Sustaining Audiovisual Edit Suites as a Learning, Teaching, and Research Resource in an Academic Library 67
   Marc Stoeckle and Christie Hurrell

7 A Tale of Two Initiatives: Developing Operational Models for 3D Printing and a Multimedia Production Studio in a STEM Library 79
   Renaine Julian, Kelly Grove, Joshua Julien, and Michael Meth

Index 95

About the Editor and Contributors 97

Figures

Fig. 0.1	A Typical Makerspace.	xii
Fig. 1.1	MADE@UF.	3
Fig. 1.2	VR for the Social Good Demo Day at MSL.	7
Fig. 1.3	MSL Staff Teaching Unity 3D Basics.	10
Fig. 2.1	Inside the AET Library.	15
Fig. 2.2	GroupSpot Student Space.	19
Fig. 2.3	GroupSpot Instruction Space.	20
Fig. 3.1	Map of Mudd Library.	26
Fig. 3.2	Example of a GIS Project.	29
Fig. 3.3	A 3D-Printed Fidget Toy.	31
Fig. 3.4	A 3D Sound Absorption Object.	32
Fig. 3.5	Number of Hours by Number of People Using the Lightboard Studio.	33
Fig. 3.6	Lightboard Video for French Class.	34
Fig. 3.7	Lightboard Video for Engineering.	35
Fig. 4.1	HoloLens Headset.	39
Fig. 4.2	3D Model of Long Tom River.	41
Fig. 4.3	3D Painted Hills Landform.	43
Fig. 4.4	Unity Screen.	45

Fig. 4.5	Wood Hologram.	48
Fig. 5.1	Floor Plan of the Creative Space.	55
Fig. 5.2	Student Using the Oculus Rift.	56
Fig. 5.3	Students Using Whiteboards and Collaborative Tables.	57
Fig. 5.4	Top Twenty-Five Tools Checked Out from Fall 2015 to Fall 2018.	58
Fig. 6.1	Use of A/V Editing Suites, July 2016 to June 2017.	69
Fig. 6.2	Audiovisual Edit Suite for Creating Audiovisual Media.	71
Fig. 6.3	Audiovisual Edit Suite for Editing Audiovisual Media.	72
Fig. 6.4	Desktop Wallpaper.	75

Introduction

Paul McMonigle

Libraries have changed tremendously over the last twenty years. They have transformed from warehouses of books and quiet study to vibrant, exciting, and sometimes too noisy places where students can find books, computers, and state-of-the-art technology. As an example, when I was an undergraduate student in the mid-1990s, the campus library was not the place to find cutting-edge technology. Computer labs were available but often lived separately, departmentally and geographically, from the libraries. With the beginnings of electronic access, libraries were working on transferring their card catalogs to online public access catalogs. If you were lucky, you could search your library's collection and access online databases using on-site terminals. Remote access through the Internet was rare and generally only available for larger public libraries. Many smaller libraries still had card catalogs for regular patron use.

Twenty-five years later, most academic libraries have large, robust IT departments. "Knowledge commons" and "makerspaces" take up many square feet of space, helping to transform libraries into "one-stop shops" for the information and creative needs of their patrons. Though this turn of events may surprise many people outside the library profession, if you take a quick look at the past, you will see that libraries have always been near the forefront of technological change.

Historically, libraries offered some of the first public access to new technologies. Servers and mainframe computers could store a large amount of information about local library inventory, giving staff the ability to quickly add and update new materials. The first commercial electronic database, "Dialog," created in 1972 in CD-ROM format, heralded a new way to store and access information.

From this point, the next step was to completely replace card catalogs with online versions. Library management systems were created to integrate the processes of acquisition and cataloging of materials. These systems evolved alongside the microcomputer, with computer labs becoming common sights at campuses across the country. Librarians began to store bibliographic data on CD-ROMs, with operating systems, hardware, and software created to encourage a total networked environment.

The rise of the Internet completely transformed all aspects of information, including libraries. Patrons could now have access to full-text materials stored off-site. Opportunities formed for true real-time distance education. Libraries could provide patrons with eBooks, electronic journals, and access to archives of informative materials. Just as important, librarians could now conduct virtual reference sessions and ensure patrons have the ability to access library materials anywhere in the world.

Another recent development dealing with the use of technology in libraries is the makerspace. Makerspaces were first conceptualized around 2005 and have been a huge success in public libraries. Academic libraries quickly adopted them as well. Most of these spaces contain items such as computer workstations, 3D printers, website creation software, high-quality scanners, audiovisual editing materials, and an arts and crafts station (Burke 2015). Figure 0.1 shows a typical makerspace in a library.

There are several motivations behind libraries' adoption of makerspaces. They exist to bring individual patrons into a space with shared resources. They provide spaces where experienced creators can teach skills and guide novice users. These areas allow for the sharing of ideas and designs. Makerspaces enable collaboration and innovation and bring multiple perspectives and skill sets together. Through tinkering with the technology, what might be considered play, patrons can discover new concepts.

Figure 0.1. A Typical Makerspace. *Flikr.*

Makerspaces have a number of effective uses in higher education. They give professors and instructors the chance to put the learning theory of constructivism into practice. Constructivism, first developed by Jean Piaget in the middle of the twentieth century, states that learners should have an active role in the process, work with peers, and have the chance to learn from their mistakes (Bates 2016). Makerspaces provide the tools students can use to solve problems and bring to life the concepts they learn in the classroom.

Makerspaces also enhance an academic library's culture of participation. Participatory culture is the idea that students are not only the consumers of information but can also be the creators (Jenkins 2009). Students have the ability to guide their own learning through the creation of projects and can share their new knowledge with others by working with their hands. As one can imagine, this is very relevant to STEM education. Students are able to use makerspaces to create prototypes of their designs and even have the ability to simulate medical conditions and body functions to test treatments. Makerspaces stimulate innovation and can even develop students' business skills through the creation of marketable products (Burke 2015).

The following chapters contain the stories of seven academic libraries in North America. Each has recently created or updated its makerspaces and technology in innovative ways to supplement the learning experience of its university. Their successes and learning experiences can give readers ideas about how to integrate technology into their own libraries. Readers can also determine how best to spend limited resources.

At the University of Florida, Samuel Putnam, the engineering librarian, has been using technologies such as Oculus Rift, HTC Vive, Microsoft HoloLens, and Unity 3D. He describes many of the initial challenges the library staff encountered when they first acquired this equipment and how they eventually overcame them. Oculus Rift and HTC Vive are both virtual reality tools that University of Florida has been using to not only augment classroom learning for both STEM and arts and humanities courses but also in community outreach projects and with local public libraries. Unity 3D is a game engine, the basic software that runs a computer or video game, that is used as a development platform for virtual reality systems. The Microsoft HoloLens, on the other hand, is a mixed or augmented reality headset. The user can still see the regular physical environment through the device; however, the lenses also have digital content projected onto them, giving the viewer the ability to see both virtual and physical reality at the same time. The digital content is used by patrons to interact with the "actual" world.

Matt Hayward, STEM librarian at the University of Texas at San Antonio, writes about "group spots," which are instruction/group spaces with high-end gaming computers and the ability to share screens in addition to other collaborative options. The name comes from the original remote sharing and communication software suite used in the space. This is an excellent example of a shared classroom/group study room, and the teaching faculty use it almost as often as the librarians.

At Northwestern University, Becca Greenstein, one of their STEM librarians, discusses her recently renovated library's use of Lightboard, GIS Lab, Maker Lab, and Solstice. She also writes about how patrons are using library-owned software packages to complete their projects. Lightboard is an easy-to-use video recording studio and includes a glass wall that users can write on or use to display slides. Solstice is a software application that allows users to share screens wirelessly with other enabled devices.

Dr. Dean Walton, the science and technology outreach librarian at the University of Oregon, writes about how faculty use the Microsoft HoloLens for their research. Walton and his colleagues use the augmented reality tool to create three-dimensional maps of landscapes to assist with future planning, understanding the aftermath of natural disasters, and analyzing an area's biodiversity for conservation efforts. To assist with the acquisition of the necessary images, the library uses remote-controlled quadcopters and other unmanned aerial systems.

Kari Kozak, the head of the Lichtenberger Engineering Library at the University of Iowa, discusses the tool library and the use of the library's Creative Space, which includes virtual reality stations, collaboration tables, modeling stations, and other options to create prototypes for engineering design. She emphasizes how the library works with the College of Engineering at Iowa to provide funding and other resources for student projects by running the Creative Kick-Start program.

Marc Stoeckle and Christie Hurrell from the University of Calgary lead readers through the renovation of audiovisual editing suites, which represent the first in-depth collaboration between their technology unit and a liaison librarian in terms of technology selection, installation, and deployment. These suites underwent an impressive upgrade with the addition of new, state-of-the-art hardware capable of running the high-end software necessary for the editing needs of students and faculty.

Renaine Julian, Kelly Grove, Joshua Julien, and Michael Meth from Florida State University proffer an overview of their high-end 3D printer lab and their video production studio. They also discuss their use of the Global Educational Outreach for Science, Engineering, and Technology (GEOSET), which is a video service used both as an educational tool and for professional scientific communication. Incorporating what had been part of a different academic department into Florida State's science library was a challenging project but one that paid off greatly in the end.

The examples contained in this book are evidence that academic libraries can use technology in multiple innovative ways to enhance the learning and research capabilities of their patrons. They show what was possible in the past and what is possible today, and they inspire the rest of us to imagine what might be possible tomorrow. Through the use of case studies, readers can explore real-life examples to determine which items are most popular, visualize how patrons are using the technology, and experience successful partnerships with campus partners. Readers will also glean ways to overcome challenges that may occur and develop ideas for solutions in their own libraries.

REFERENCES

Bates, B. 2016. *Learning Theories Simplified . . . and How to Apply Them to Teaching.* Los Angeles: Sage.

Burke, J. 2015. "Can Makerspaces Work in Academic Libraries?" *Proceedings from the 2015 Association of College and Research Libraries Conference.* Portland, Oregon.

Jenkins, H. 2009. *Confronting the Challenges of Participatory Culture: Media Education for the 21st Century.* Cambridge, MA: MIT Press.

Chapter One

Engaging Users with Technology at the University of Florida Libraries

Samuel Putnam

Virtual reality (VR) is establishing an increasingly large role in the public sphere. VR, as experienced through a corresponding head-mounted display, was first introduced by Ivan Sutherland in a paper titled "Head-Mounted Three Dimensional Display" while at the University of Utah in 1968, though his research originated during his time at the Massachusetts Institute of Technology (Sutherland 1968, 757). Sutherland's groundbreaking work of combining a head-mounted display (HMD) with a computer is seen as the earliest iteration of VR as defined today. Over the past fifty years, researchers have been working to improve upon this virtual experience. In the past five years, virtual reality hardware has gone from inaccessible technology confined to arcades or academic labs to a ubiquitous technology that can be used with a smartphone and special lenses. Google searches for "virtual reality" have steadily increased along with availability over the last five years (Google, n.d.). Companies, such as Facebook (parent company of Oculus), HTC, Microsoft, and Magic Leap, have invested serious capital in expanding virtual reality in the marketplace. According to International Data Center, a market intelligence provider, augmented reality (AR)/VR spending is projected to increase from $11.4 billion in 2017 to nearly $215 billion by 2021 (Bolkan 2017).

As VR expands its reach, libraries of all kinds are acquiring these new technologies in an effort to support the evolving information needs of their patrons. Libraries have responded by experimenting with ways to provide access to virtual reality technology, both hardware via head-mounted displays and VR-capable computers and software including development platforms and immersive experiences. Understanding the rapidly developing VR landscape can complicate an already complex information landscape for library professionals, especially those interested in implementing VR programs. Although the history of VR is long and complex, understanding the current, relevant components is considerably less cumbersome.

RECENT BACKGROUND OF TECHNOLOGY

In 2012, Oculus launched a successful Kickstarter campaign that secured $2.5 million to produce their first head mounted display (HMD), the Development Kit 1 (Oculus, n.d.). In the following two years, Oculus, which had been recently acquired by Facebook (Facebook 2014), began developing a VR system that would be its most accessible to date, the now-ubiquitous Oculus Rift. The release of the Oculus Rift and consequent releases of new VR platforms generated interest in VR beyond those developing and designing VR experiences. Consumers without strong technological skills were now able to use VR in their homes and businesses. Although Oculus led the way with an early consumer-friendly VR system, several other companies were observing VR's rise and developing their own VR projects simultaneously.

HTC Vive was released in 2016, the product of a partnership between HTC and the Valve Corporation (HTC 2016). HTC primarily produces hardware, beginning with laptop computers before finding success with smartphones. Valve Corporation's first product was the wildly successful video game franchise Half-Life; eventually Valve moved on to create Steam, a software distribution platform used by millions of gamers around the world (Case 2002).

Concurrently, smartphone makers such as Samsung and Google began designing headsets to transform their phones into HMDs. In 2014, Google simplified the product down to paper and lenses with the rollout of Google Cardboard in 2014 (Google 2014). Microsoft entered the market in 2016 with an alteration to the traditional virtual reality HMD (Microsoft News Center 2015). Microsoft HoloLens premiered as one of the first mixed reality headsets to enter the market. Mixed reality differs from virtual reality. First, users can still see their physical environment through the headset's lenses. However, those lenses have digital content projected onto them, allowing the physical and digital environments to be viewed simultaneously. Mixed reality takes it a step further in that the digital content interacts with the user's physical environment. The interaction between the physical world and digital content is achieved as the HoloLens uses various cameras and sensors to interpret a space for its digital content. The HoloLens cost $3,000, limiting the device's adoption by casual users but opening the door for other developers.

After the HoloLens, start-up companies such as Magic Leap have entered the market with their own spin on augmented and mixed reality headsets, with a lower price tag. As these consumer-friendly VR systems emerged, select academics began to consider VR's impact across disciplines.

SPACES AND TECHNOLOGY LENDING

Marston Science Library (MSL) at the University of Florida (UF) considers supporting VR development and use a core tenet. The basis for the VR space and lending program is outlined in the UF Libraries Strategic Directions to "deliver diverse and up-to-date technology resources to foster innovation, enhance learning and improve collaboration (George A. Smathers Libraries 2014)." MSL began its foray into supporting virtual reality in 2014 with the purchase of the Oculus Development Kit 2 (DK2). Although MSL librarians were excited to be incorporating VR services, MSL established barriers to access due to the fear of damaging the expensive equipment. Access to the Oculus Rift DK2 was limited to in-library use only. DK2 could be used at one computer in MSL's MADE@UF space, a computer lab focused on supporting mobile app development. Figure 1.1 provides an image of the MADE@UF space. Patrons were required to sign a one-time user agreement and received a special sticker on their student ID in order to check out an access card to use MADE@UF and the DK2.

The DK2 also offered limited options for development software, training opportunities, and immersive experiences. Platforms such as Unity and Unreal, both complex game engines, were some of the only platforms available to develop VR experiences. These same game engines, on which developers

Figure 1.1. MADE@UF. *Photo taken by Barbara Hood.*

created the immersive content, did not offer documentation, directions, or tutorials at the time. VR experiences were also limited as the marketplace had only been open for a limited time and most companies working in VR development were still in their infancy. MSL's staff effort was also significantly higher in the beginning of the program due to the lack of options. Library staff spent time combing through forums and message boards to troubleshoot problems, often only to discover there was no resolution. The most egregious example of wasted staff time occurred when Oculus pulled support for Mac; at the time, MADE@UF used Mac computers exclusively. This resulted in staff making the decision to shelf the DK2 until funding for VR-capable PCs could be acquired. The combination of limited support for early VR adopters, exhausted personnel resources, and barriers to access were all a part of the growing pains associated with beginning this new space and program.

Although MSL librarians were still excited about the potential for the new program and space, the difficulties in establishing the technology lending program and MADE@UF were evident. The space and technology saw low use in all areas. During library outreach events, staff learned that students and faculty had no knowledge of MADE@UF despite using other library spaces or resources. Eventually, the library's more savvy patrons discovered the often-empty space, but only to use it as a quiet study space when library study rooms were booked. By 2016, MSL librarians understood that changes needed to be made to the space and services. Two strategies were identified: cultivate potential partnerships with faculty interested in VR and remove barriers to access hindering patrons from using the technology.

Initially, the VR program was designed for patrons to use the technology within the library in the MADE@UF space. The space allows patrons to use VR-ready computers equipped with dedicated graphics cards, powerful processors, sufficient RAM, and several USB and HMDI ports. The dedicated graphics card is the primary barrier for patrons attempting to use VR hardware on their personal computers. Computers need a NVIDIA GTX 1060, AMD Radeon RX 480, or greater. These graphics cards either need to be self-installed or come as a part of a high-end gaming computer. MADE@UF provides nine computers capable of running VR hardware. Five stations are permanently set up for VR use: four for the Oculus Rift and one for the HTC Vive. The other four computers can be used with a patron's personal VR equipment or to develop VR on the software provided by the library.

The computers are also equipped with the relevant software to develop VR. Unity 3D and Unreal Engine are the most popular game engines. The UF legal department was only able to come to an acceptable licensing agreement with Unity, which comes installed on the machine. Other game engines can be installed by individual users, although each computer is wiped after the library closes each day. Unity 3D is the most popular development platform with the patrons. Students use it to develop class and personal projects, while faculty tend to work on the Unity platform. Unity's primary advantage is that it is free for educational purposes, allowing students to create in the MADE@UF space or download to a personal computer. MADE@UF also provides the software development kits (SDKs) in Unity to deploy to any platform. Experiences built on Unity deploy to twenty-seven platforms, including Google Cardboard, Oculus Rift, SteamVR (platform for HTC Vive), PlayStation VR, Samsung Gear VR, Windows Mixed Reality (platform for Microsoft HoloLens), Google Daydream, Apple AR Kit, Google AR Core, and Vuforia (Unity, n.d.).

This design seemed to benefit both patrons and the libraries. The library purchased expensive equipment that required pairing with expensive computers built for VR use. The library also desired to preserve and protect this potentially fragile equipment by keeping the equipment in MADE@UF. Patrons, who are typically college students without access to or the means to purchase expensive computers built for VR use, could use the space provided. However, the program and space's low use ran counter to MSL's assumption. MSL librarians decided on a different approach to increase use.

Beginning in fall 2018, MSL began a pilot program to circulate a portion of VR technology outside of the library for seven days. MSL librarians decided to design a program that catered to our small audience of dedicated VR users. Although MSL would still provide the computers and technology in MADE@UF, MSL would also allow students who were highly involved in development to gain more time with the technology while determining a location on their terms. Librarians identified three HTC Vives and one Microsoft HoloLens for the pilot to circulate these items outside of the library. The equipment was placed in a reservation system using LibCal to allow patrons to book ahead of time and see future availability.

Since the implementation of the new policies, each of the three HTC Vives circulated outside the library for one-week loans on average of eight times per device for the fall semester, spanning from August 20 through December 14, 2018. Each HTC Vive was circulated on average for 56 of 116 total days. This was an improvement on the eight loans for in-library use of HTC Vive from January 1 through August 20, 2018. The Microsoft HoloLens circulated sixteen times, accounting for 112 days of the 116-day semester, improving on the ten loans for in-library use from January 1 through August 20, 2018. The entire MSL team is excited that this equipment is being used at a greater rate and will seek to add more VR technology that can circulate outside of the library.

PARTNERSHIPS

In addition to the changes to the lending program, MSL librarians began to cultivate partnerships with faculty, student groups, and other stakeholders on campus. The early users of the VR technology were a small group of excited students who had recently created a club on campus, GatorVR. GatorVR is a student club that meets weekly to discuss VR, lead trainings and workshops, host speakers, and complete one VR project each semester. In 2016, MSL agreed to host GatorVR events in MADE@UF, pending confirmation with librarians each semester. This partnership helped MADE@UF establish itself as the unofficial hub for VR development on campus and brought the first consistent use of the space and lending program. The libraries cosponsor their workshops and speaker events by advertising through campus partners and providing refreshments. GatorVR members typically lead the workshops and invite any speakers, although MSL has also led a few applicable workshops and invited speakers. GatorVR members also receive a survey each year to provide feedback on the space and suggestions for new VR technology purchases. The survey results factor heavily in decisions and are often used in grant applications to justify new VR purchases. Examples of purchases suggested by GatorVR include HTC Vive, Google Daydream, Samsung Gear VR, Magic Leap One, and Leap Motion Controller.

Access to VR equipment is a boon not only for patrons in student clubs but also for faculty as a means to enhance course content. Librarians have partnered with several faculty members across campus to integrate VR into university courses. Most prominently, the VR for the Social Good course asks students to form teams to develop VR experiences to pitch ideas to outside groups. Approximately 125 students take the VR for the Social Good course each semester, splitting into twenty-five teams of five students; each team takes on a different pitch and works with the outside groups to realize their vision by the end of the semester. Students display their final projects, a complete VR experience, at a Demo Day event with attendees from the entire university community (Figure 1.2). Along with GatorVR, VR for the Social Good students are heavy users of the library's VR equipment because the computer science department and journalism department, which both list the course as part of their major, do not provide hardware for the students to develop their VR projects (VR for the Social Good, n.d.).

In addition to supporting courses that focus on virtual reality development, MSL has also partnered with faculty across disciplines to implement virtual reality into their curriculum. These partnerships include faculty teaching courses in astronomy, English, biology, medieval studies, classics, and others.

In astronomy, virtual reality experiences are easy to discover as several developers have glommed on to the idea that space exploration would make

Figure 1.2. VR for the Social Good Demo Day at MSL. *Photo taken by Barbara Hood.*

an interesting immersive experience. "Overview: A Walk through the Universe" was voted by Viveport, HTC Vive's storefront, as the best educational game of 2018 and is even narrated by the European Space Agency astronaut Jean-Francois Clervoy (Overview, n.d.). Unfortunately, MSL was unable to use most games restricted to the Oculus and Viveport storefronts due to legal issues with licensing agreements. Thus, MSL librarians needed to discover open-source options. This led to the discovery of NASA's immersive experiences. The first experience MSL librarians discovered was NASA's Exoplanet Excursions VR Experience (NASA, n.d.). NASA describes the experience this way: "Take a guided journey through the amazing TRAPPIST-1 star system in VR, known to be the home of 7 Earth-size exoplanets orbiting a star that is only a little larger than Jupiter. This experience is based on the best current understanding of what these worlds could be like given their sizes, densities, and proximity to their star. While the planetary images are artistic extrapolations, the relative sizes and positions are all portrayed accurately."

The Space Telescope Science Institute (STScI), an organization operated for NASA, provides WebbVR: The James Webb Space Telescope Virtual Experience (STScI, n.d.). This experience is based on the James Webb Space Telescope that orbits Earth just beyond the moon. Participants can explore the full expanse of the solar system as well as the Orion Nebula.

Faculty benefit from the NASA experiences due to NASA's authority and credibility in astronomy; other third-party experiences can require additional vetting, especially when considering their use as core course material.

MSL librarians also work with faculty from microbiology and cell science to use VR in the Molecular Genetics course. Students in this course use VR to help them visualize proteins involved in gene expression and DNA replication and repair. The course uses UnityMol, a molecular editor, viewer, and prototyping platform built on the Unity game engine. UnityMol describes the product as "a stand-alone viewer capable of displaying molecular structures, surfaces, animated electrostatic field lines and biological networks with powerful, artistic and illustrative rendering methods" (Chavent, n.d.). UnityMol can read Protein Data Bank files, along with several other formats, and deploy them from Unity to the Oculus Rift and HTC Vive for users to interact with. The program can also work with a Leap Motion controller, a device that works in conjunction with VR headsets to control and manipulate the virtual environment using hand gestures. Students from the course were formed into project groups, each responsible for different proteins. Groups made reservations with MADE@UF and completed their necessary work as part of a larger project.

Outside of the sciences, MSL also worked with graduate students from the English department to implement VR into a course titled Issues in Twentieth-Century American Literature and Culture: Thinking Outside the Book. The course featured a VR experience titled Queerskins: A Love Story. Queerskins was created for the Oculus Rift and utilizes the Oculus Touch controllers to immerse students in a virtual storytelling experience. Queerskins takes place in the early 1990s and follows a mother as she processes her estranged son's death from AIDS. Students from the class, approximately thirty in total, received a group training session on using VR at MSL in preparation for the assignment. MSL librarians also worked with our IT department to install Queerskins on the VR devices for a time-limited period, which satisfied the agreement with the author. Students thoroughly enjoyed the VR experience with some remarking in evaluations that it was their favorite part of the class. The graduate student teaching the course was also pleased to be able to include this rare instruction experience in his doctoral dissertation.

In classics, students use VR technology to tour ancient civilizations, both the ruins left by them and artistic renderings of their former glory. These experiences offer interaction with these civilizations without physically traveling to them or constructing a time machine. Experiences such as Rome Reborn and Unimersiv allow students to explore these locations (Rome Reborn, n.d.; Unimersiv, n.d.). Interactions with antiquities rendered as 3D objects in digital space connect students to busts and statues as well as common items, including casks, bowls, and other household objects. Examples of these projects include Rekrei, formerly Project Mosul, which "is a crowdsourced project to collect photographs of monuments, museums, and artefacts damaged by natural disasters or human intervention, and to use those data to create 3D representations and help to preserve our global, shared, human heritage" (Rekrei, n.d.). These projects create immersive experiences that are no longer available in the physical world but can be re-created in immersive digital experiences.

The Center for Medieval and Early Modern Studies uses Google Earth VR to explore German cities in an immersive manner. Google Earth works for both the HTC Vive and Oculus Rift and allows full mobility with use of the corresponding controllers (Google, n.d.). Users can walk or fly through locations around the globe, allowing tours of historical locations without the burden of time and cost associated with traveling abroad. Students in these courses participate in virtual tours conducted by their instructor either synchronously or asynchronously depending on class size. One specific drawback of Google Earth VR is its inability to read KMZ files, the file type used to save tours in Google Earth and Google Maps. Therefore, individuals need to re-create their Google Earth or Maps tour in the Google Earth VR platform as it cannot be converted from the former to the latter.

MSL staff also work with the university's Center for Instructional Technology and Training (CITT), which is comprised of instructional designers who serve the majority of the faculty on campus. CITT houses and runs its own virtual reality lab specifically for faculty to use. Faculty work with CITT staff to experience VR and design coursework around corresponding experiences. However, CITT does not provide a lab space for students to participate in these experiences. Therefore, MSL staff work with these faculty and instructional designers to use library technology and space to deploy these experiences to their courses.

Outside of the university, MSL librarians use the VR collection in outreach with local schools, community groups, and public libraries. Local school and community groups visit MADE@UF and have the opportunity to learn about and experience virtual reality. These groups usually attend a short presentation taught by a librarian about the history and applications of virtual reality. Participants then explore educational virtual reality experiences.

MSL staff host Girls' Tech Camp, which is an annual technology camp for middle school girls. The camp focuses on introducing and educating young girls about science, technology, engineering, and math (STEM) topics used in STEM careers. This weeklong adventure allows the participants to explore emerging technologies through creative projects. Campers spend each of the five days at camp focused on a different STEM area. Each summer, one of the days is dedicated to virtual reality, with the projects ranging from creating a simple game in Unity 3D or exploring augmented reality through the use of HP Reveal (formerly Aurasma). Figure 1.3 shows staff teaching campers the basics of Unity 3D.

Librarians at MSL also host workshops about using VR in libraries for public librarians in north central Florida. Through partnerships established in

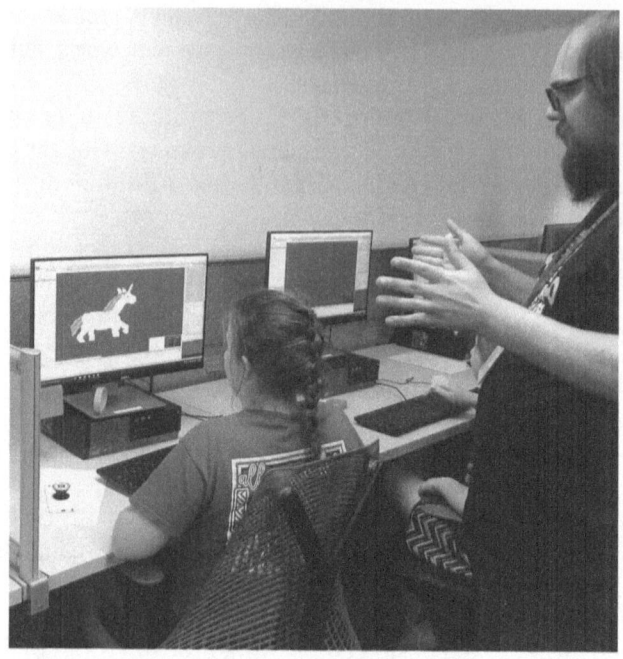

Figure 1.3. MSL Staff Teaching Unity 3D Basics. *Photo taken by Samuel R. Putnam.*

the Northeast Florida Information Network, MSL librarians have taught librarians from Alachua County, Jacksonville, St. Augustine, and other areas about implementing VR into the life of the library. These workshops are specifically designed to give hands-on experience and create a community of interest for VR in libraries around the region.

ACCESSIBILITY

A large drawback of experiences that use the Oculus Rift and HTC Vive is that the technology is not accessible to all individuals, depending on a patron's disability or discomfort with VR. These barriers cannot be easily resolved and require faculty to consider alternate methods for instruction to ensure an inclusive course. One resolution to this issue is to use screen recordings of VR experiences and allow patrons to experience VR in a less immersive but more accessible environment. Software such as NVIDIA Shadowplay and Open Broadcaster Software allow instructors to record and narrate VR experiences and export them into standard video files (NVIDIA, n.d.; Open Broadcaster Software, n.d.). Although patrons will not be able to fully participate in an immersive VR experience, they will still be able to participate in the course.

NEXT STEPS

Virtual reality's expansion from irrelevant to ubiquitous has pressed librarians into a new field in order to serve the evolving academic community. As virtual reality technology continues to advance and prices continue to fall, libraries will need appropriate hardware and software as well as relevant experience in order to keep up with this changing information landscape. Whether you are serving faculty or undergraduate students, supporting VR will create opportunities and add value to any library.

REFERENCES

Bolkan, Joshua. 2017. "Report: VR and ART to Double or More Every Year Through 2021." *Campus Technology*, August 7, 2017. https://campustechnology.com/articles/2017/08/07/report-vr-and-ar-to-double-each-year-through-2021.aspx.

Case, Loyd. 2002. "Valve Changes Online Gaming Rules." *PC Magazine*, March 22, 2002. https://www.pcmag.com/article2/0,2817,41291,00.asp.

Chavent, Matthieu, and Marc Baaden. n.d. "Home." Accessed January 11, 2019. http://www.baaden.ibpc.fr/umol/.

Facebook. 2014. "Facebook to Acquire Oculus." Facebook press release, March 25, 2014. https://newsroom.fb.com/news/2014/03/facebook-to-acquire-oculus/.

George A. Smathers Libraries, University of Florida. 2014. *Strategic Directions, 2014 (Complete)*. Gainesville, FL: George A. Smathers Libraries, University of Florida. http://ufdc.ufl.edu/IR00004144/00004.

Google. n.d. "Google Earth VR." Accessed January 10, 2019. https://vr.google.com/earth/.

Google. 2014. "Cardboard: VR for Android." Google I/O, June 26, 2014. https://www.google.com/events/io/schedule/session/603fe228-89c5-e311-b297-00155d5066d7.

Google Trends. n.d. "Virtual Reality - Explore - Google Trends." Accessed November 30, 2018. https://trends.google.com/trends/explore?date=all&geo=US&q=virtual%20reality.

HTC. 2016. "Vive Now Shipping Immediately from HTC, Retail Partners Expand Demo Locations." HTC press release, June 7, 2016. https://www.htc.com/us/newsroom/2016-06-07/.

Microsoft News Center. 2015. "Microsoft Redefines the Laptop with Surface Book, Ushers in New Era of Windows 10 Devices." Microsoft press release, October 6, 2015. https://news.microsoft.com/2015/10/06/microsoft-redefines-the-laptop-with-surface-book-ushers-in-new-era-of-windows-10-devices/.

NASA. n.d. "NASA's Exoplanet Excursions VR Experience." Accessed January 13, 2019. http://www.spitzer.caltech.edu/vr.

NVIDIA. n.d. "ShadowPlay." Accessed November 30, 2018. https://www.nvidia.com/en-us/geforce/geforce-experience/shadowplay/.

Oculus. n.d. "Oculus Rift: Step into the Game – Kickstarter." Accessed January 15, 2019. https://www.kickstarter.com/projects/1523379957/oculus-rift-step-into-the-game.

Open Broadcaster Software. n.d. "Open Broadcaster Software Home." Accessed November 30, 2018. https://obsproject.com/.

Overview. n.d. "Overview: A Walk through the Universe." Accessed November 30, 2018. https://www.overviewexperience.com/.

Queerskins. n.d. "Queerskins - A Haptic Experience for Virtual Reality, and an Interactive Installation." Accessed January 11, 2019. http://vr.queerskins.com/.

Rekrei. n.d. "About Rekrei | Rekrei." Accessed January 10, 2019. https://projectmosul.org/about.
Rome Reborn. n.d. "About/Contact | Rome Reborn." Accessed January 11, 2019. https://romereborn.org/content/aboutcontact.
Space Telescope Science Institute (STScI). n.d. "WebbVR Available for Free Download." Accessed December 1, 2018. https://jwst.stsci.edu/news-events/news/News%20items/webbvr-available-for-free-download.
Sutherland, Ivan E. 1968. "A Head-Mounted Three Dimensional Display," In *ProceedingA-FIPS 1968 (Fall, Part I) Proceedings of the December 9–11, 1968, Fall Joint Computer Conference, Part I (San Francisco, California)*, 757–64.
Unimersiv. n.d. "Learn About Us - Unimersiv - Virtual Reality Training Solution." Accessed January 10, 2019. https://unimersiv.com/about-us/.
Unity. n.d. "Unity." Accessed November 30, 2018. https://unity3d.com/.
VR for the Social Good. n.d. "VR for the Social Good Initiative at the University of Florida - Home." Accessed November 30, 2018. http://www.vrforthesocialgood.com/courses.html.

Chapter Two

John Peace Library and the Applied Engineering and Technology Library, University of Texas at San Antonio

Matt Hayward

The University of Texas at San Antonio (UTSA) is a doctoral-granting research institution in one of the nation's most populous cities, serving more than thirty-two thousand students across two campuses. UTSA is one of the top Hispanic-serving institutions in the nation (UTSA, n.d.) and ranks in the top five young universities (i.e., under fifty years old) in the United States and the top seventy-five worldwide according to the World University Rankings (Times Higher Education 2018). UTSA's cybersecurity program was ranked number one in the United States according to an HP Enterprise Security–sponsored research report (Ponemon Institute 2014).

With tens of thousands of students divided between two campuses, more than one library is a necessity. Located in the city's metropolitan center, the Institute of Texan Cultures and the Downtown Library hold many of the libraries' special collections and serve academic programs based at the downtown campus, respectively. The main campus, located on the rapidly expanding northwest side of San Antonio, also has two dedicated libraries. John Peace Library (JPL), UTSA's main library, is central to campus and houses the majority of UTSA Libraries' more than eight hundred thousand physical books, as well as the special collections. The Applied Engineering and Technology (AET) Library, a remote, bookless library, is located in a location convenient to science and engineering students. The AET Library will be further discussed later in this chapter.

UTSA Libraries employs a staff of just over a hundred but serves over seven thousand students per day, accounting for more than 1.7 million visits per year. Because the libraries are primarily funded by student fees, spaces and services are focused on meeting the needs of UTSA students. Meeting ever-evolving student needs requires the library to keep up with library trends and continually monitor student space and service use through user testing and anecdotal input. Dean Hendrix, dean of libraries at UTSA, frequently says that "everything [at UTSA Libraries] is in constant beta," conveying the libraries' principal charge of being responsive to students' needs.

Persistent focus on student needs has led to implementing many innovative technologies across the libraries, but especially at JPL. Some ideas inevitably fall short of expectations, but thanks to the flexibility of the "constant beta" leadership stance, failures are viewed as opportunities to grow and better understand student needs.

TECHNOLOGY AT JOHN PEACE LIBRARY AND DOWNTOWN LIBRARY

John Peace Library and Downtown Library each offer common pieces of popular technology, such as laptop checkout, KIC scanners, device charging stations, and iMac design studios. In addition to common technology, including laptops and calculators, both libraries offer multimedia equipment including digital single-lens reflex camera (DSLR), video, GoPro cameras and accessories, AR/VR goggles, smartphone gimbal and video rig, and multimedia recorders, players, and projectors. Both libraries also employ a few innovative entry pieces to welcome patrons, such as iPad podiums configured to allow students to instantly find and reserve study rooms in the library. This service is also available through the libraries' website. Additionally, strategically placed Raspberry Pi–connected monitors are used to display digital signage and convey to patrons how many computers are currently available and where in the library to find open computers.

JPL is open twenty-four hours a day during the average work week and features two computer classrooms that can each be split in half using hideaway partitions. The Library Computer Classroom and GroupSpot seat fifty and one hundred students, respectively, and are equipped with laptops for each student as well as two instructor laptops. The GroupSpot will be discussed in more depth later in the chapter.

With all of the tech running at UTSA Libraries, it is fortuitous to have an embedded systems and informational technology department. In addition to a full systems staff available during normal business hours, Office of Information Technology (OIT) staff are stationed at the information desk during all open hours to assist students, staff, and faculty with technology issues. Having OIT ever-present in the library alleviates student distress over finding urgent tech support, hastens issue resolution for library staff, and eases a fraction of the burden on campus OIT.

THE APPLIED ENGINEERING AND TECHNOLOGY LIBRARY

In 2010, UTSA Libraries opened the doors to the AET Library. Dubbed "the nation's first completely bookless academic library" (Rapp 2010), AET is located in the Applied Engineering and Technology building, central to other science and engineering buildings on campus. Rather than stacks, AET offers access to UTSA Libraries' quickly growing collection of electronic resources, including over ninety thousand e-journal subscriptions and nearly 1.7 million eBooks. The STEM librarian holds weekly office hours in AET to provide research assistance and reference consultations. At just under 2,300 square feet and with a capacity of only seventy-five people, the diminutive library may have a small footprint, but it nevertheless has a large impact on UTSA's STEM students.

Amenities at AET include eight all-in-one computers (AIOs), three group study rooms, a glass wall that can be written on with dry-erase markers (available for checkout), and tech gear lending, including laptops, scientific and graphing calculators, headphones, chargers, and display adapters. The AIOs are maintained by the Engineering Department OIT and loaded with specialized software, such as Autodesk, ArcGIS, Matlab, SolidWorks, Visual Studio, and WMS. Each study room has space for up to six people and is equipped with a dry-erase board, writeable glass walls, and a forty-two-inch monitor that students can use to display their laptops for collaborative work. Figure 2.1 provides a look at AET study rooms.

The library is extremely popular among science and engineering students, who fill the library to capacity and beyond during finals and other major

Figure 2.1. Inside the AET Library. *Photo taken by Matt Hayward.*

exam and project weeks. Some use the modeling and mathematical software on the AIOs to create designs and simulations for class projects. Others reserve the study rooms, so they know the space will be waiting for them, then use the libraries' display adapters to connect to the forty-two-inch monitors in order to view informational videos, collaborate on papers, perform statistical analyses, model prototypes, and work on other projects in which they can benefit from working together on a single screen. Many patrons check out dry-erase marker kits to write mathematical, physical, and chemical equations and diagrams across the glass walls around the library. Other patrons use the moveable tables in the lobby area to assemble appropriate-sized workstations for their study groups, which can range from two or three up to ten or more students, all working together toward a single goal.

Despite being well liked, AET, like everything else at UTSA, is also in "constant beta." One example of this at AET is eReader lending; this was offered at the inception of AET and was expected to be a hit. Unfortunately, the cost of maintenance and repair combined with low circulation numbers and increasing laptop and tablet ownership among students led to abandoning eReader checkout. Even the physical space of the AET is beta. In 2017, the AET was moved to a lower level of the AET building in a more open and visible setting.

GROUPSPOT

The most popular technology at the UTSA Libraries is the GroupSpot classroom at the JPL Library. While the technology in GroupSpot is not extraordinary, when the classroom first opened in 2014, it was an immediate hit with students. Then, once the room was opened for instruction, it became equally popular with library instructors and other faculty.

The initial proposal for the space specified that it would be used as a media lab. Fortunately, this not-fully-developed depiction was enough for the library to obtain funding from the Hearst Foundation in the form of a $150,000 grant. UTSA Libraries began investigating media labs in other academic libraries, looking for inspiration. After discovering the Student-Centered Active Learning Environment with Upside-down Pedagogies (SCALE-UP) concept from North Carolina State University, the planners decided that the principles of the SCALE-UP design would be the basis for the UTSA design.

The SCALE-UP concept was initially designed for physics classrooms consisting of one hundred or more students, but the key components of the concept are transferrable across disciplines and equally applicable for smaller, but still large, class sizes. The most important characteristic for GroupSpot, taken from the SCALE-UP model, is the focus on a simple but versatile classroom design that promotes active learning and collaboration in an interactive learning environment.

While researching collaborative software to incorporate into the classroom, GroupSpot and TeamSpot software, by Tidebreak, were decided upon. It was with this decision that the room got its name—GroupSpot. When the classroom was first opened, there was no marketing. Following the example of the Virginia Tech library's SCALE-UP launch, it was decided that there would be a soft opening to allow the library to observe student use of the space without policies or guidance in place. The only advertising came from a sign outside the propped-open doors and guides about the collaborative software placed on each table for direction. After the soft opening in April 2014, it was clear that GroupSpot was a hit with the students.

The space was so popular that students revolted when the library closed off the classroom for instruction. Following a two-week barrage of negative calls, emails, suggestion box comments, and complaints to library staff by students who wanted to use the room for study, it was decided that one side of the classroom would be left open for student use except in limited cases where the entirety of the space is required.

A grand opening event was held shortly after the start of the fall semester and featured popcorn, music, dancing, a demo of databases on the new computers, and a T-shirt door prize for the first hundred students. As hoped for, there was a line of students looking for free T-shirts at the door thirty minutes before the event started.

At its core, GroupSpot is a large computer classroom with projection screens at both ends, a movable room divider with whiteboard surfaces, and twenty group workstations. The room layout, laptops for each student, and collaborative software are what make the space so sought after by instructors and students alike.

When divided, as it remains the majority of the time, each side of the room holds an instructor podium and laptop, two projection screens, and ten workstations. The workstations are each equipped with five laptops and a desktop CPU that is attached to a forty-six-inch table monitor. These CPUs, and their respective monitors, can be remotely accessed from the five laptops at each workstation. Laptops were chosen over desktop computers so that patrons have greater space to use their own laptops or work on tasks that do not require a computer. In addition to displaying on the projection screens, the instructor laptop can also be displayed on the forty-six-inch monitors mounted at each workstation. This is helpful for students with vision difficulties and for those following along with instructors on their laptop, in order to avoid having to focus on a laptop screen and the instructor's demonstration at the same time.

One of the most important aspects of the space, from the planners' perspective, was to keep it simple. Ensuring that hardware and software operations are user-friendly helps prevent frustration, which ultimately increases patron use and reduces the burden on systems staff. Unfortunately, the GroupSpot and TeamSpot software, which were first used to enable the collaborative display, in addition to being costly, were found to be cumbersome. Using the software typically required a minimum of ten to fifteen minutes of training for unacquainted users. Due to this, the programs were replaced with NetSupport School and TightVNC, respectively. NetSupport School, which was much more cost-effective than GroupSpot, and the TightVNC freeware could both be more easily explained via a tutorial document, short video, or a few minutes of hands-on training.

NetSupport School allows the instructor to communicate and share his or her screen with the monitors at each workstation. NetSupport offers many other learning and instructional features, such as messaging, monitoring student work, testing, and other assessment tools, but those features are used very infrequently if at all.

TightVNC is a remote desktop software that gives patrons the ability to work collaboratively on the desktop CPU from the five individual laptops. TightVNC emulates the desktop CPU in a window on each connected laptop. Within this window, the patrons at a given workstation can all simultaneously control the mouse and keyboard input for the desktop CPU and monitor. This setup allows users to work collaboratively on assignments and research on the big screen for all to see while performing individual research and minor tasks on their individual machines.

During weekdays, the partition is deployed to divide the room into two separate spaces for up to fifty students per side. Side A (Figure 2.2) is available for students to use, while Side B (Figure 2.3) is reserved for instruction. Most evenings, weekends, and throughout finals week, the partition is opened and students are allowed to use the entirety of the classroom for individual or group study.

The collaborative technology and versatile design of GroupSpot have made it just as popular with faculty as it is with students and library instructors. The popularity led to adoption of a policy that during the first nine weeks of the fall and spring semesters, the room is only open for librarians to reserve for library instruction. Starting in the tenth week, faculty and staff from other departments may reserve Side B by contacting a subject-specialist librarian or completing a reservation request form. This policy ensures that subject librarians have access to the classroom during the first half of the semester, when library instruction tends to be heaviest. Occasionally exceptions are made for faculty use of the class during the first nine weeks as long as they are deemed to not interfere with library instruction, for instance, during off hours or last-minute reservations for hours that are still open. Currently the room is reserved via a Microsoft Outlook calendar, but plans are in place to move to 25Live, an institution-wide reservation system.

Figure 2.2. GroupSpot Student Space. *Photo taken by Matt Hayward.*

Library instruction in the room ranges from fairly typical computer classroom use, such as demonstrating search techniques while allowing patrons to try out their own searches on the laptops, to more engaging information literacy group activities, including Library Jeopardy, citation round-up, and think-pair-share activities. Since the majority of UTSA library classes are one-shot, fifty- to eighty-five-minute classes, focused on introducing library resources and information literacy, it can be challenging to take full advantage of the collaborative technology that the room has to offer. The seating arrangement of the room contributes to student interaction, promoting group discussion and collaboration, even at times when the space is being used as a traditional computer classroom.

A music marketing course that relies on OER materials uses the room, and the music librarian introduces the students to blogging. During the first class, students create accounts for the OER blog on a Humanities Commons platform and then work in groups to identify what makes a blog comment appealing. The students then list elements of comments that they consider successful or unsuccessful. The comments are then written on the whiteboards for all to see and discussed as a class in a conversation to demonstrate the grading rubric for the ongoing blog assignment. The technological features of the room help students collaboratively browse and read blogs and make it easy for the instructor and students to provide help with registration and technical issues regarding the platform.

Despite more advanced technological features of the room, the whiteboard walls are one of the most used items by many librarians. For example, one librarian frequently uses activity prompts for students to review several

Figure 2.3. GroupSpot Instruction Space. *Photo taken by Matt Hayward.*

peer-reviewed journals. The journals are laid on each group's table, and after reviewing the journals the students are to write a word or phrase on the dry-erase wall that describes peer-reviewed literature based on what they see. These terms are then used, along with the definition of peer review, to convey to students what sets peer-reviewed work apart from popular or trade publications.

A recurrent freshman academic inquiry class taught in GroupSpot begins with demonstration of database searching and concepts that students can follow along with on their own laptops and finishes with students putting together sources for their final group presentation. The students, seated with their respective groups and working together, first perform general searches about their overall topic to determine what facets of the topic each will cover. Following this format, each student spends a few minutes on his or her laptop looking for peer-reviewed sources that discuss the overall focus of the topic. Later in the class period, the big monitors are used to bring together the sources each student has found, and the group creates a bibliography that will be used to form the basis of the essay.

Faculty use of the room is much more variable as they prefer to utilize GroupSpot for focused, specific class sessions, which often work better for incorporating the room's tech functionality. Simple classes, such as library research sessions and résumé-writing workshops, are most common, but the room also sees a variety of other class styles.

The room has been used for rhetoric classes where each table served as a station to work on individual speeches, with students moving from table to table until each group had analyzed every speech. Art classes have been conducted where Google Docs were collectively built for social protest artists using the TightVNC software.

Imagine the Possibilities is another innovative class held in GroupSpot by faculty in the education department. The purpose of the class is to introduce prospective teachers to innovative technology that can be used for learning, for instance, Google Cardboard and augmented reality books. Students are divided into groups, each seated at a table with a different technology item that could be used in teaching. The students watch an informational video about their technology on the big monitors, then experiment with the tech, using the laptops for some modules, and discuss how it could be implemented in an educational environment. When the buzzer sounds the students rotate, á la musical chairs, to the next table to try out the next tech item.

One of the more entertaining activities in the room came from an engineering lesson on developing schematics. Students were divided into groups of five and assigned to a station. Each station served as a lab bench where students worked in groups to disassemble items and create schematics for the items using TightVNC so that all could view results on the large monitors. The circular seating arrangement, large viewing screen for the group's schematic, and ability to push some of the laptops out of the way all contributed to the success of this lab.

A math instructor uses the room for an Excel class where student groups work on the large monitor to create spreadsheets with integrated statistical formulas. The monitor and collaborative software obviously work great for the task, but the instructor said the reason she chooses to reserve GroupSpot for this class is the arrangement of seats around the central monitor, which "work a lot better than the other labs where [students] seem isolated and would not communicate as much."

Student use of the room also varies greatly, with individual students looking for a less quiet place to use a library computer or study with friends to chemistry students using the collaborative software and whiteboards to virtually build molecules or draw electron configuration diagrams. The space continues to be so popular that occasionally students still wander into the instruction side for individual and group study, even while instructors are actively using the space for library instruction or standard course classes.

CONSIDERATIONS

While the room is very popular and fairly user-friendly, as with any design, there are a few points to keep in mind for other libraries considering implementing a similar space. The room requires a bit more regular maintenance by both systems and custodial staff. Although the computers restart with a clean image after each reboot, they still perform slowly if not properly maintained. Since library staff are less available and visible in the GroupSpot classrooms, students are often more prone to be physically careless with the laptops and other movable items. This is less of a problem at UTSA where the library houses its own OIT support staff but could be taxing for libraries without internal support.

The side of the classroom that is left open for students can be quite loud at times. The information desk is just outside of the room at UTSA, so the volume can be monitored by staff at the desk. It's often purported that the loudness of the room is due to the initial soft opening, during which students were given free rein, and the grand opening, which was more akin to a party than a library event. This drawback could potentially be reduced by eliminating individual study in the space, but that would likely result in a second student revolt. Other ways of dampening the sound transfer need to be considered.

FUTURE DIRECTIONS

The UTSA Libraries' constant beta stance means that while the current arrangement and state of technology may be appropriate and successful, there is also opportunity to revise. An excellent example of such a modification was the abandonment of TeamSpot over the course of this chapter being written. TeamSpot was a small computer lab that was opened concurrently with GroupSpot and offered some similar collaborative technology to promote group work. In observing how students used the TeamSpot space, it became obvious that students preferred the less-conspicuous location and quieter study area for individual or group quiet study. In TeamSpot, the collaborative technology was rarely, if ever, used. To provide the students with the space they truly wanted and alleviate concerns with further maintenance and tech support needs, the collaborative technology pieces were removed from the room. Large monitors connected to a single laptop were left at each workstation, but the other library laptops were removed and replaced with engineering department computers that allow for more engineering study and provide additional software choices for other students.

Beyond the current composition, plans are also in the works to reconfigure the third floor at JPL, where the majority of UTSA open stacks are located. Although no formal plans have been developed, the groundwork is currently being laid for a substantial renovation that would decrease on-site holdings in order to provide an adaptable, reconfigurable study space offering more innovative study tools and resources. Some of the pieces being assessed for this space include virtual and augmented reality tools, 3D printing and other maker technology, and multimedia content creation and production tools.

ACKNOWLEDGMENTS

Thanks to Jan Kemp, Richard Quini, and Rachel Cannady for providing essential background information and guidance in putting this chapter together.

REFERENCES

Ponemon Institute. 2014. *2014 Best Schools for Cybersecurity: Study of Educational Institutions in the United States*. Traverse City, MI: Ponemon Institute.

Rapp, D. 2010. "UTSA Announces 'Bookless Library.'" *Library Journal* 135, no. 17.

Times Higher Education. 2018. "Young University Rankings 2018. Times Higher Education." Accessed September 26, 2018. https://www.timeshighereducation.com/world-university-rankings/2018/yo...!/page/0/length/25/locations/US/sort_by/rank/sort_order/asc/cols/stats.

UTSA. n.d. "Academic Highlights." Accessed July 11, 2019. https://www.utsa.edu/about/glance/marks-of-excellence.html.

Chapter Three

Lightboard and ArcGIS and Solstice, Oh My!

Becca Greenstein

The Seeley G. Mudd Library at Northwestern University contains most of the science and technology collections on campus. It underwent renovations from March 2016 to August 2017 and reopened at the beginning of the fall quarter 2017. The redesigned space occupies most of the second floor of Mudd Hall and contains many pieces of cutting-edge technology, all of which, with the exception of computers and a plotter, were not in the old space. In its first academic year of operation, the space has seen a number of students, faculty, and staff using the physical space, physical and digital collections, and various pieces of technology. This chapter will discuss use statistics and patterns for computers and software, the plotter (poster printer), geographic information system (GIS) lab, Maker Lab, Solstice projection technology, and the lightboard/One Button studio. Examples of use will be included in some of the sections. A map of the space, which indicates where the pieces of technology are located, is shown in Figure 3.1.

COMPUTER USE

Mudd Library has a total of thirty-two public computers (twenty-two PCs and ten Macs) in two areas in the library. The computing area by the circulation desk, which includes three printers and the plotter, has twelve PCs. The computing area by the classroom has ten PCs, ten Macs, and one printer. The old library had twenty-two total public computers. Anyone with Northwestern credentials can log in to the computers.

At peak times, all ten Macs and twenty-one out of twenty-two PCs were in use. The total use numbers and total use time for all three quarters are

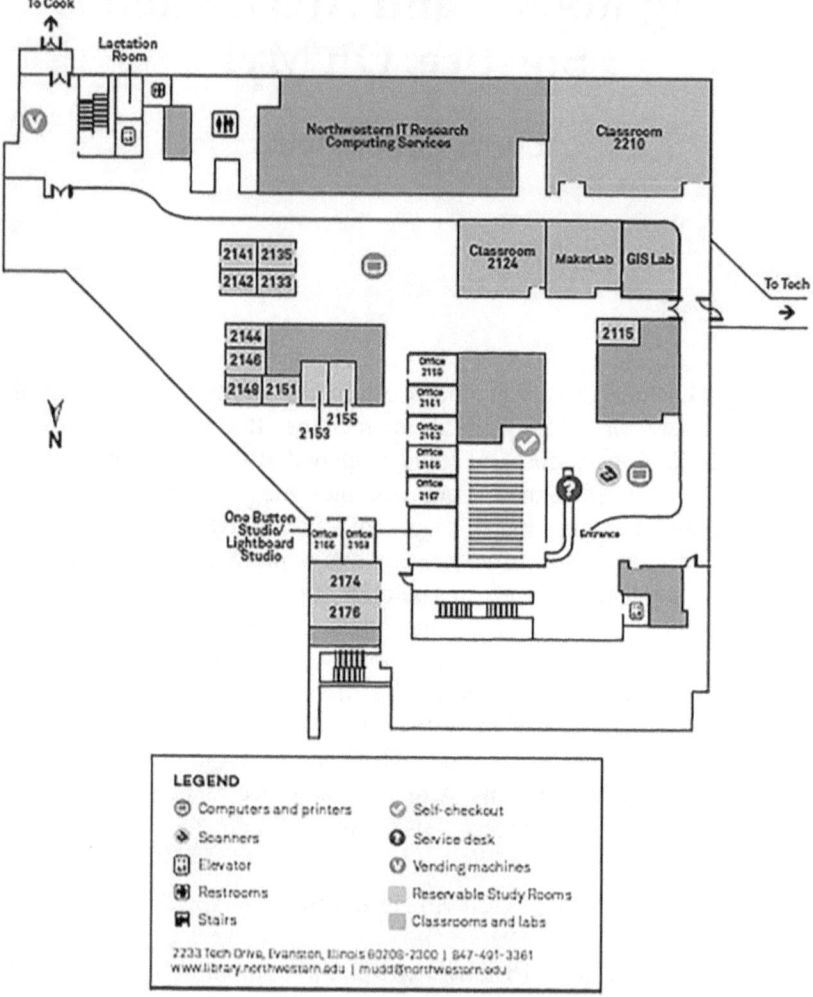

Figure 3.1. Map of Mudd Library. *Created by Mudd Library.*

robust and are relatively consistent across quarters. Quarterly use data for individual computers were also gathered. Use data for the ten Macs and for the ten PCs near the classroom are relatively similar across individual machines for the three quarters and across all machines in total. Most of the computers were used between two hundred and four hundred times each quarter. Staff have noticed that patrons don't like to sit next to each other, so patrons might sit at Mac 2, then Mac 4, and so on. For the twelve PCs in the computing area near the circulation desk, use differs drastically across individual machines. In general, PCs 7 to 12, which are closer to the library entrance, have more uses than PCs 1 to 6, which are close to the glass wall. The glare from the sun might also disincentivize patrons from sitting at PCs 1 to 6. PCs 7 to 12 were used, on average, five hundred to seven hundred times per quarter, while PCs 1 to 6 were used, on average, two hundred to four hundred times per quarter. PC 2 was also under repair for much of the spring quarter, which explains its low use counts. PC 7 is the closest computer to the library entrance, which explains its high use numbers. These statistics do align with what staff have noticed from observing patrons at the computers.

Average weekly use for individual computers was also analyzed. Most of the twenty computers near the classroom were used, on average, between fifteen and twenty-five times per week. For each computer, the use is relatively consistent across quarters, with a number of the computers experiencing higher use in the spring. Perhaps more students knew about Mudd Library and its resources in the spring quarter; it will be interesting to see if this trend continues into the fall. For the twelve PCs near the circulation desk, use is again dependent on location, with the six more accessible PCs (PCs 7 to 12) having a higher average weekly use (roughly forty to sixty times per week) than the less accessible ones (PCs 1 to 6, roughly fifteen to twenty-five times per week). This is in accordance with what librarians have observed: patrons will often print a document in the computing area near the circulation desk and then leave rather than sit and study for a long period of time.

PLOTTER

Located in the computing area by the circulation desk, the plotter is an Océ ColorWave 600: a self-service, wide-format printer. Patrons use the plotter to print posters for conferences and class presentations; sometimes many members of a single class print their posters on the plotter. Cost is $2.50 per square foot of printed material, payable through Northwestern affiliates' NUprint printing accounts. More information about the plotter is available in the plotter research guide (http://libguides.northwestern.edu/plotter).

In the period from September 1, 2017, to June 15, 2018, 306 individuals sent 407 jobs to the plotter. These jobs used a total of 3,330 square feet of paper. Anecdotal evidence from a number of people suggests that the plotter is a valuable tool and they appreciate its ease of use.

GIS LAB

The GIS Lab is located down the hall from the first computing area, close to the bridge to the Technological Institute. It has four workstations with dual monitors that have ArcGIS software for GIS and data visualization projects. Patrons are welcome to use the lab on their own or work with a library staff member on their project in the lab. More information can be found on the Geospatial Services website (https://www.library.northwestern.edu/libraries-collections/government-collection/maps-gis/index.html). The GIS staff team started holding four office hours per week during spring quarter.

Use of the GIS computers varied slightly for each quarter; each computer averaged roughly 130 uses per quarter. Despite the addition of office hours, use did not increase overall during the spring quarter. Since the GIS team will continue to offer office hours this coming academic year, it will be interesting to continue to track use into the fall. It is important to note that it is impossible to know who is logged on to the computers—GIS staff or students.

The GIS team conducted 302 total consultations during the 2017–2018 school year. An interesting example is when a faculty member in the Feinberg School of Medicine was interested in the number of emergency department visits for gunshot wounds in areas including and surrounding Chicago. He and the GIS specialist mapped the information by zip code of where the gunshot wound victims lived (not where they were shot), and the map was then color coded based on the number of emergency department visits. Another GIS project is shown in Figure 3.2. The researcher, a faculty member in the business school, was interested in coffee bean production in Uganda. He and the GIS specialist mapped the type of coffee bean by region. They color coded the map based on type of coffee bean.

MAKER LAB

Mudd's Maker Lab is right next to the GIS Lab. It opened in January 2018 and contains three 3D printers and one 3D scanner. More information can be found on the Maker Lab website (www.library.northwestern.edu/libraries-collections/mudd-library/technology-spaces/maker-lab.html). Mudd is open to all Northwestern affiliates and is the only Maker Space on campus that is open to all, unlike The Garage (thegarage.northwestern.edu/resources/prototyping-lab/) and the Segal Design Institute (design.northwestern.edu/about/design-facilities/prototyping-lab.html). Mudd library is currently offering a mediated printing service; patrons need to have a consultation to use the technology and/or submit a project request for staff to print.

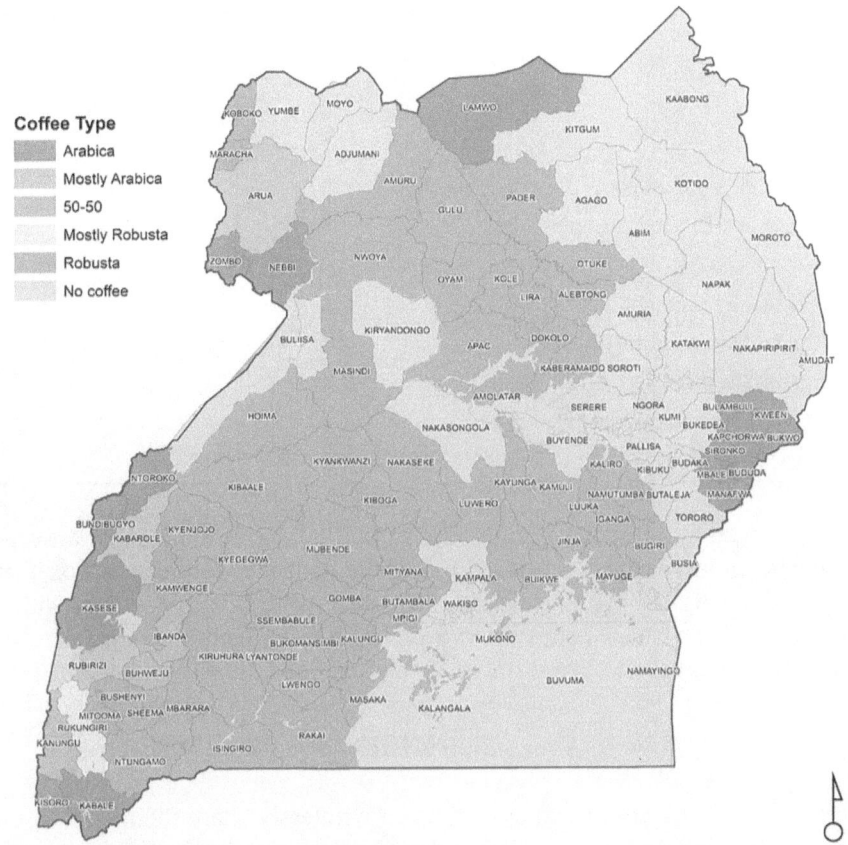

Figure 3.2. Example of a GIS Project. *Photo taken by Ameet Morjaria.*

From January to August 2018, the six Maker Lab staff members printed 229 projects (including internal library jobs), using 9,083 grams of filament. They conducted twenty-one project consultations for more in-depth projects and helped sixteen faculty, twelve graduate students, forty-three undergraduate students, and forty-two staff members with projects. The distribution of projects by department or major (for those with more than two projects) is shown in Table 3.1. The majority of users were in the STEMM fields (science, technology, engineering, math, and medicine). With the addition of open lab hours in the fall quarter, it will be interesting to see how Maker Lab use changes.

An example of a 3D-printed object, a fidget toy, is shown in Figure 3.3. Another example, a sound box, is shown in Figure 3.4. The researcher who designed the sound box, a member of the Sound Arts and Industries depart-

Department/Major	Number of Projects
Neurobiology	17
Engineering	14
Physiology	8
Physics	7
Mechanical Engineering	8
Chemical and Biological Engineering	8
Library	6
Biomedical Engineering	5
Center for Fundamental Physics	4
Computer Science	4
Manufacturing and Design Engineering	3
Radio/TV/Film	3

ment, wanted to construct a sound absorption box with the highest absorption/mass ratio possible to deaden noise; the goal was to create a box that provided the highest sound isolation using the lowest weight possible, with a maximum size of two inches by two inches by two inches. The researcher printed out uniquely designed sound panels and lined the box with them.

SOLSTICE

Solstice is a software that allows users to wirelessly share their screens on any Solstice-enabled display. Users download an app and enter the unique key for the display they want to project to. Multiple users can share their screens on one display.

Each of Mudd's twelve study rooms, located around the corner from the Maker Lab, is equipped with a Solstice-enabled display. Users can project slides, collaborative documents, or helpful formulas on the display. Both of Mudd's active learning classrooms are also equipped with Solstice technology. The small classroom is next to the Maker Lab, has five Solstice screens, and can fit twenty-four participants. The large classroom is outside the main library space, has ten Solstice screens, and can fit sixty participants. Instructors have the option to show their screen on the main monitor or on all monitors, have the participants each share their own screen, or have one group's display projected on all of the monitors.

Solstice is heavily used in the study rooms. While statistics are unavailable, anecdotally, the author has seen some patrons project a single shared document on the screen to work collaboratively on a project. Others practice for a presentation, either by themselves or with others, and project slides on

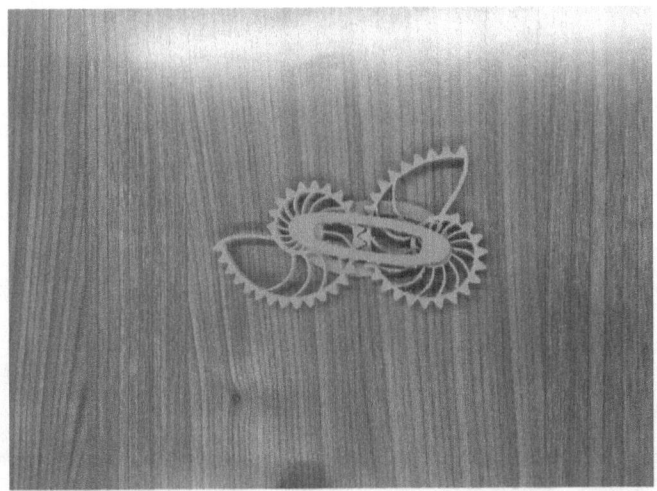

Figure 3.3. A 3D-Printed Fidget Toy. *Photo taken by Angie Mah.*

the screen. Still others appreciate the ability to see their work on a screen larger than a laptop screen. Using Solstice in the classrooms allows for active learning opportunities and less sage-on-a-stage instruction. Instructors can lecture, let groups project their work onto each screen, and then highlight the work of a successful group on all the screens. Participants can look at whichever screen is most convenient for them, allowing for a less stressful learning experience.

LIGHTBOARD AND ONE BUTTON STUDIO

The lightboard/One Button studio opened in November 2017 and is located down the hall from the group study rooms. The lightboard is a glass wall that is pumped full of light and used for recording video lectures. Users can write on the glass wall while facing the audience. Videos are saved to a flash drive and can be immediately distributed. The One Button studio allows participants to video record themselves talking (with or without slides) and save the video on a flash drive. Common applications of the One Button studio include making a demo video, practicing a presentation, practicing for an interview, or practicing a monologue. More information about the lightboard can be found on the lightboard website (http://lightboard.info/); more information about the studio can be found on the library website (https://www.library.northwestern.edu/visit/technology/index.html).

Figure 3.4. A 3D Sound Absorption Object. *Photo taken by Ted Quiballo.*

From September 1, 2017, through August 30, 2018, users with 261 unique email addresses used the lightboard studio for a total of 1,186 hours. Breaking use down by affiliation, self-identified undergraduates used the studio for 447.4 hours, self-identified graduate students used the studio for 264 hours, self-identified staff and faculty used the studio for 332.5 hours, and users who did not self-identify used the studio for 142 hours. It is unknown whether the studio was used for One Button recording, lightboard recording, or studying, but the space is getting a fair amount of use. One notable statistic is that patrons reserved the studio, on average, 7.4 days ahead of time. They reserve the small study rooms in Mudd, on average, 4.3 days ahead of time, pointing to the usefulness of the studio (the large study rooms are reserved, on average, 11.5 days ahead of time, probably because teaching assistants hold office hours there).

Figure 3.5 shows how many hours groups of various sizes were in the lightboard studio. Groups of one to five people predominantly reserve the studio. As it would be logistically difficult to have fifteen people record in the span of 2.5 hours, reservations of this size are likely for a tour or introduction to the space. It is promising that patrons are using the space in groups, most likely for group projects or collaborating on a lightboard or One Button video.

Use was low during the first few months of fall 2017 but spiked in November when it was ready for public use until winter break. In January 2018, use climbed steadily until May and dipped when the summer started. It

Group Size	
1	223.5
2	286.5
3	176.9
4	111.5
5	105.5
6	31.5
7	4.5
8	13.0
9	1.5
10	6.0
15	2.5
Field is blank	223.0

Figure 3.5. Number of Hours by Number of People Using the Lightboard Studio. *Created by Rebecca Greenstein.*

will be interesting to see if use stays at the same level for the fall and winter quarters for the next school year.

An example of someone using the lightboard is shown in Figure 3.6. Dr. Rey, a French professor at Northwestern, is developing a series of "flipped French" videos that her students watch before class; when they come to class, they are ready to apply the material in group work or activities. She can indicate various parts of sentences by pointing at the words on the slides. Lightboard videos work well in language classes because students can see the way professors' mouths move when they pronounce unfamiliar words. They are also good for STEM classes, where instructors frequently write equations or refer to figures during class. Figure 3.7 shows Dr. Peshkin, a professor of mechanical engineering and the inventor of the technology, using the lightboard to make a video for an engineering class.

The Mudd circulation desk also has a slide advancer, lapel microphone, lightboard markers, and USB drive available for check-out for use in the studio. The general use trend is relatively similar to the use trend for the space itself; use peaks in early 2018 and then decreases as time goes on. As with use for the studio itself, it is unknown if the person who checked out the object actually used it. It also can't be determined if it was used by one person or multiple people. As the lightboard markers and lapel microphone are not materials that patrons would normally have, it makes sense that these items are checked out more frequently than the slide advancer and USB drive.

MARKETING

Mudd Library published a blog post (https://www.library.northwestern.edu/about/news/library-news/2017/fresh-mudd-at-last-north-campus-library-reopens.html) describing the reopening of the updated library. The reopening was also promoted on social media (https://www.facebook.com/NorthwesternLibrary/, https://twitter.com/NU_LIBRARY, and https://twitter.com/NUSTEMLibrarian). Students quickly made use of the space itself.

A number of other library events and services took place in Mudd throughout the academic year. Exam relief activities are offered each quarter since Mudd reopened. In February, there was a faculty open house where staff provided tours and demonstrations of the technology in Mudd. For Love Your Library Week in April, staff hosted a button-making session in the Maker Lab. All these events were promoted via social media. When the

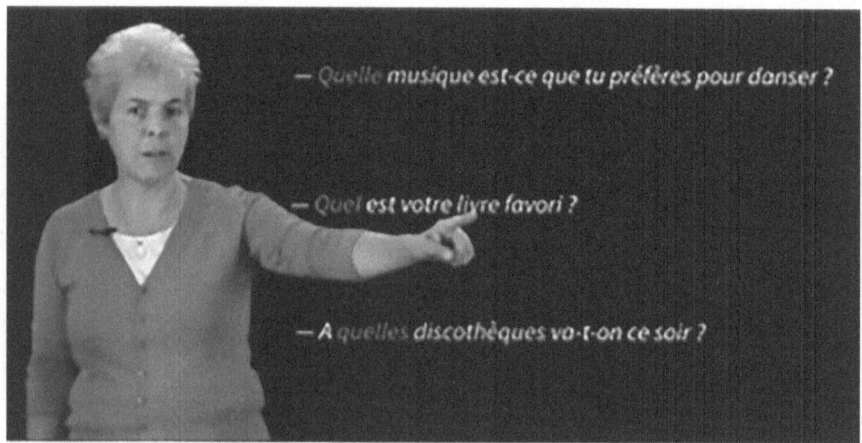

Figure 3.6. Lightboard Video for French Class. *Photo taken by Christiane Rey.*

Figure 3.7. Lightboard Video for Engineering. *Photo taken by Michael Peshkin.*

lightboard/One Button studio and Maker Lab opened, these were advertised via social media, and the Maker Lab was also promoted on digital signage boards in Mudd. Digital signage advertising for the Maker Lab and lightboard studio is planned.

For the lightboard, the author made a quick video outlining its capabilities, which can be found on multiple library webpages (https://youtu.be/f36YRnNUodw). She has also presented about the lightboard at a few conferences to spread the word, both at Northwestern and elsewhere, as well as writing a blog post about it (https://www.jove.com/blog/library/northwestern-librarian-discusses-campus-teaching-tech/). Due to her promoting one of the presentations on social media, a librarian at another institution learned about the lightboard. The authors sent her information about the lightboard, and she submitted a proposal to her institution to build her own.

CONCLUSION

Since its reopening in fall 2017, Mudd Library has seen extensive use of both its space and various pieces of technology. As the Mudd Library heads into its second academic year of renovated operation, it will be interesting to see if the robust use patterns seen already will continue and if other use patterns will emerge.

ACKNOWLEDGMENTS

The chapter author is very grateful to her colleagues for providing data, anecdotes, project examples, and helpful feedback. Thanks are due to Danielle Cotrone, Melissa Jacobi, Basia Kapolka, Angie Mah, Lauren McKeen, Mike Perry, Gina Petersen, Ted Quiballo, Kelsey Rydland, Cory Slowik, and Bob Trautvetter in the libraries, and Joseph Feinglass, Avery Makel, Ameet Morjaria, Michael Peshkin, and Christiane Rey for permission to use their work.

Chapter Four

The Holographic Landscape

3D Modeling for the HoloLens

Dean Walton

This chapter introduces the concepts of creating holograms of 3D landscape models as a way of exploring the power of this technology using faculty experiences. All equipment is available from the Prices Science Commons and Research Library at the University of Oregon.

Academic libraries are one of the prime places for university patrons to experience new technologies regardless of their discipline. While there are some technologies that remain hidden in the labs of specific disciplines, other technologies, such as mass spectrometers, can be used for not just areas of chemistry but also archeology, art history, and other fields. Likewise, geographic information systems (GIS) are used in marketing, history, biology, geography, political science, and almost every other field. Access to tools that can easily cross disciplines, particularly those that can be utilized in the digital humanities, will foster new research in interdisciplinary and multidisciplinary areas. Libraries function as neutral areas on a campus and can easily host technology shared among researchers and students from multiple departments and fields. However, it does come with a cost, not only of the technology but also the effort to implement the technology, particularly if it is not yet widely used in a particular field. Therefore, libraries and librarians that do support the sharing of new technologies need to invest some time and research on how these tools are currently used and could be used in the future. This is true for the use of augmented reality (AR) media and viewing this media via devices such as the HoloLens.

Augmented reality, in contrast to virtual reality (VR), allows one or more viewers to see digital representations of objects placed in specific spatial orientations without being cut off from the physical environment. For example, a user can place a digital representation of a bridge within a viewed part of a 3D map. In this example, both a 3D landscape and the bridge could be digital holograms. In a video relating to Microsoft HoloLens, several architects look at an architectural model of a building on a table before one of the participants uses a hand command to make the building large enough to walk into to see the internal view of the building (Microsoft HoloLens 2016; National Futur 2016). Cipresso and colleagues (2018) wrote a comprehensive overview contrasting VR and AR systems that is beyond the scope of what is covered here.

In the augmented world, also known as mixed reality, viewers do not lose full visual and/or audible contact with their surroundings. This can prevent much of the disorientation and motion sickness associated with VR. In VR, the user can experience visual cues that contradict what the person's vestibular system is reporting to the brain. There are a number of anecdotal stories of people falling down while using VR. At the 2018 LITA Makerspace Technology Interest Group session of the annual meeting of the American Library Association, several librarians reported that they were so concerned about the issue that they had patrons sign safety waivers excluding the library from liability before allowing patrons to use VR tools or games. Thus, AR is a more likely candidate for patron acceptance. However, the development of devices that can shift between AR and VR through changes in screen opacity may make this issue moot in the near future.

One of the first academic AR uses that included use of holograms was a HoloLens project for teaching human anatomy and physiology. Microsoft and Case Western Reserve University presented holograms of the human body as separate models of the skeleton, muscles, organs, and nervous system. The viewer is able to walk around the holographic body as though it were a real body and review the hologram from any angle. This provides the HoloLens viewer a life-size image of a body and the opportunity to review its anatomical features on many levels. Case Western Reserve faculty member Mark Griswold reports, "You see it [the torso hologram] truly in 3D. You can take parts in and out. You can turn it around. You can see the blood pumping—the entire system" (Case Western Reserve University 2015). Gaming is another use of the technology, and Microsoft created environmentally aware games where the HoloLens can detect structures, such as doors and furniture, in a specific room within the game. While others are exploring pedagogical or artistic uses, the majority of published academic or scientific work describing uses of the HoloLens relate to medical purposes for visualizing organs and surgical methods (Agten et al. 2018; Jang et al. 2018; Moreta-Martinez 2018; von Haxthausen et al. 2018; Wang et al. 2017; Wiebrands et al. 2018).

At the University of Oregon, faculty members have been using the HoloLens (Microsoft, n.d.), an AR tool, to model landscapes for planning, understanding natural disasters, and performing biodiversity/conservation analyses as ways of better understanding its research potential. In most cases, this is done via the capture of aerial imagery from a quadcopter or other uncrewed (unmanned) aerial vehicle (UAV) in conjunction with structure from motion (SfM) technology (Kawanishi et al. 2013; Snavely et al. 2008). This suite of technologies creates a powerful system for landscape analysis (Carmichael 2016; Erat et al. 2018; Fonstad et al. 2013; Golparvar-Fard and Savarese 2011; Guo and Gao 2013; Milanesi 2017; Wang et al. 2018; Zmarz et al. 2018). Figure 4.1 shows a HoloLens headset.

Faculty at the University of Oregon first started using the HoloLens for various landscape analyses with the development of a model of the Haitian National Palace a few years after the January 12, 2010, magnitude 7.0 earthquake just outside the capital city of Port au Prince. This was the first attempt at solely using imagery posted online by others to create the model. Unfortunately, a good working model could not be generated. The review of the images used to make the model revealed that aftershocks and rescue work shifted many of the sections of the collapsed palace in the series of images used. Given all of these subtle but real shifts of the location of objects between images taken on different dates, the photo-alignment software could not generate a single model palace. Instead, the software superimposed multiple 3D models of the palace in the same 3D space.

Researchers continued testing types of landscape analyses with the digital re-creation of a rock outcrop in the area of Monterey, California (Walton 2015). Due to the geomorphology of the Monterey Bay, upwelling cold water brings food to the coastline, supporting a vast array of wildlife. The

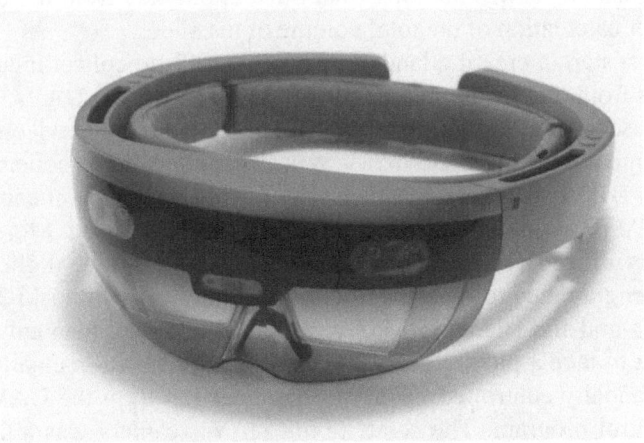

Figure 4.1.   HoloLens Headset. *Photo taken by Dean Walton.*

interface of the ocean and the land creates a zone of fog at the coast. This zone supports a set of rare lichens that grow on the rocks just in this fog zone. The initial goal of the landscape model was to better understand the microhabitats that support this rare lichen. Three-dimensional models, such as those described can be rotated in 3D space, revealing areas of rock overhang that may form the specialized habitat where this lichen can thrive.

In March 2014, a landslide in Oso, Washington, killed forty-three people. To assist in visualizing the landslide, researchers created files for 3D models and files for the placement of the landslide model in Google Earth (Walton et al. 2017a). The initial model was based on photos taken by the author at the landslide site and from other landslide images posted on online news sites and image galleries, such as Flickr. The model was georeferenced using Agisoft Photoscan (Agisoft, n.d.) software described later in this chapter.

One of the important powers of the SfM technology is the time frame in which the work can be done to generate the model. For the Oso landslide, only thirty minutes was needed to capture enough imagery to make the initial model, and the work was completed at almost no cost. This is in contrast to the thousands of dollars needed if a researcher wanted to create a similar model with LIDAR data. The author used a handheld sixteen-megapixel camera (Pentax K30) to capture this initial imagery and brought along a UAV to capture additional aerial imagery.

A second strength of these 3D models is the software's ability to detect changes in a set of models. If a boulder has shifted slightly between two 3D models of the same landscape, the software can color code the object that shifted as well as highlight the original spot. This allows the user to easily see what moved and measure the distance that it moved. The software also has the ability to calculate the volume of the object that moved. In the example of the Oso landslide, it was obvious what moved, but data from the model also allowed for calculation of the total volume of the slide.

The first step in creating landscape holograms is to collect imagery. This imagery is from real landscapes and is often obtained from UAVs. Researchers often use several UAVs (Walton 2014). A Blade 350 quadcopter with a camera gimbal carrying a GoPro IV was first employed to collect imagery. Later, two DJI quadcopters, a Mavic with a twelve-megapixel camera and a Phantom IV Pro with a twenty-megapixel camera were used. More recently, researchers utilized a scratch-built UAV with an open-source flight controller that was programmed to fly a specific set of flight lines (Siminski 2018). The DJI UAVs and the Blade 350 UAV were either flown manually with the camera set to take a picture every three seconds or flown manually with the camera manually controlled via a Wi-Fi connection from the UAV to a cell phone control program. The scratch-built UAV's camera was a GoPro and was utilized in the same fashion as that of the Blade 350.

There are several types of software that can be used to program the flight pattern of a UAV in order to collect imagery. Ardupilot and OpenPilot are common open-source software products, while a popular professional-grade software platform is Pix4D (Pix4D, n.d.). Pix4D also provides other services that will be described in the next section. One noted problem with programmed flight lines is that they can induce systematic errors. This happens when a small error or artifact in an image is amplified as multiple images with the error are combined together.

In a recent research situation, researchers utilized the Pix4D software to create a 3D model of a fluvial section of the Long Tom River in Oregon for a nonprofit group (Walton 2017b). The group holds an annual fair on parts of the property, while the rest of the year the land is managed for conservation purposes. In this case, the flight software controlled a Phantom IV UAV. Pix4D's online service was used to create a 3D model of a section of the river's path and its adjoining forest. The model was presented at the fair and displayed as a video of the rotating image on a 2D cell phone screen. It would have been better to show the model in a form where it could be rotated in 3D space as needed, but the limited electrical power and Internet services in the area during the fair made this too great a challenge. Instead, the model was displayed as a screen capture video on a cell phone showing the landscape rotating in 3D space. It worked, and the demonstration was well received by the target audience. A still of the image is shown in Figure 4.2.

Researchers have also worked on a larger landscape of another site for display on the HoloLens (Walton et al. 2017a; Walton 2018). This model was of an eroding hillside on a badlands geologic formation (Martínez-Murilloa et al. 2013). These badland areas are thought to erode at different rates from the neighboring non-badlands areas. In this case, the area in question is

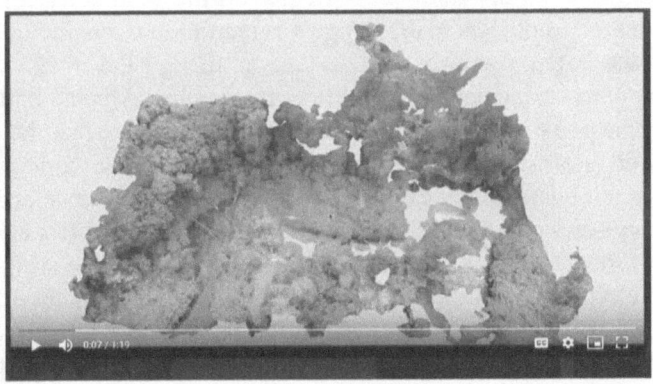

Figure 4.2. 3D Model of Long Tom River. *Photo taken by Dean Walton.*

just south of the Painted Hills Unit of the John Day Fossil Beds National Monument, known for its colorful badland topography. Researchers at the University of Oregon are investigating the erosional processes taking place in the area and are interested in creating a 3D model to better understand microhabitats that could support several rare plant species.

The following is a general description of the full process of obtaining the imagery needed to create this landscape hologram for the HoloLens. For the Painted Hills model, researchers used 945 semioverlapping images of the landscape captured either by a UAV or from a handheld camera. This model was presented at the Society for Conservation GIS's 2017 annual meeting and was demonstrated with the HoloLens in hand for viewers to evaluate.

Once a set of overlapping landscape images is available, the researcher can implement a technique known as structure from motion (SfM) or photo alignment (Kawanishi et al. 2013; Snavely et al. 2008). Computer programs such as Agisoft Photoscan will randomly select an image from the set and find the nearest match. The program can then build outward by adding images and mathematically calculating the position and orientation of the camera used to take a specific image that shares the geometric features of the starting (seed) photograph. As the software adds more and more images and the position of the camera that took each image is calculated, the computer program generates a 3D model of the subject of the image—in this case, a landform. This model initially forms as what is termed a point cloud where the software can place a particular point viewable in multiple images into 3D space. Given hundreds to thousands of these points, a 3D image emerges as a pointillistic image of the landscape. The power of this technique is that the X, Y, and Z axes of the model become orthorectified, such that there is little 3D distortion of the object and that any object with known dimensions in the model can be used to measure the size of any other object in the model. This is most widely done using a GoPro camera or other extreme wide-angle cameras that tend to distort objects greatly on the peripheral edges of the image compared to objects in the image's center. Often, this includes images that show the horizon as a curved surface as though the image was taken from a near outer-space perspective. This curvature is corrected in the model.

The coarse point cloud serves as a review tool to ensure that the process is working well. Poor-quality images or images with varied content, such as people, sky, clouds, shadows, and vehicles that move from place to place between pictures, can result in poor alignments that create errors. Reflective surfaces can result in the software forming 3D structures that are just reflections off buildings or water surfaces. These entities can certainly exist as real 3D structures, but their location is not at the point of the reflective surface. The system will calculate the place where each photograph was taken and create a marker at that point in a 3D space environment on the computer screen. A user can rotate the point cloud object and the camera markers to review the developing model. If a particular camera location appears to be wrong, or if a specific photographic image seems to be causing a problem, the specific images can be removed.

Once the images are oriented and the points of the point cloud appear to create a faint image of the desired object, the system will reevaluate the images and create a secondary dense point cloud. The formation of the secondary point cloud can take many multiples of the time needed to create the coarse point cloud. It can take hours to days to make a dense point cloud from a set of images. In work looking at a rock outcrop in an area that supports rare lichens, the researchers used thirty-six images to create a 3D object of the outcrop. A coarse alignment and creation of a coarse point cloud took under ten minutes on a computer with thirty-two gigabytes of ram and using an Intel i5-7600 quadcore processor set and an NVIDIA GeForce GTX 1060 6GB graphics card. The Painted Hills landform 3D model was built using 945 images and took around twenty-four hours to make the dense point cloud (Figure 4.3). At this point, the dense point cloud should resemble the item or landscape the user is trying to model. The Photoscan program again allowed users to rotate the object in 3D space to review it.

The next step was to create a mesh out of the point cloud. This is similar to the connect-the-dots coloring books that children use. The computer connects the dots in 3D space, creating a 3D surface of thousands of triangular facets. For a landscape, users often will only have its upper surface, but for smaller objects that can be viewed in real life from all sides, the mesh will cover all parts of the object if they are visible in the photographic set. The user now has a digital representation of an object that will serve as the basis for the HoloLens hologram or as an object in video games.

3D objects for holograms can be created using computer-assisted design (CAD) programs such as Rhinoceros 5, Fusion 360, AutoCAD, SolidWorks, or Blender. This can be as simple as using a drawing tool to create a circle

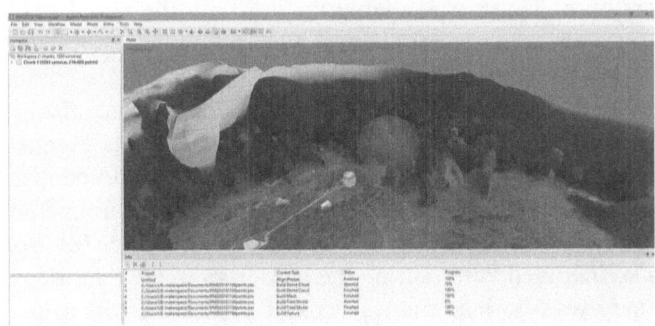

Figure 4.3. 3D Painted Hills Landform. *Photo taken by Dean Walton.*

and then rotating the circle 360 degrees to form a sphere or drawing a square and then pulling on the square's surface such that it is extruded or stretched out into a cube or rectangular box. Each of these 3D objects can now be turned into holograms.

In the initial exploration of creating holograms for landscape analysis, the researchers created a model with a high level of detail. The first model was comprised of a mesh of about five million facets. Being unsure about the computational prowess of the HoloLens, researchers simplified the mesh of the model using a command in the Rhinoceros 5 CAD program. They continued with this process, sequentially decreasing the number of facets in the model by half, for several iterations. Each iteration removed a level of detail from the model. When they reached a model of only ten thousand facets, the model took on the appearance of a blocky video game landscape instead of a real landscape. At this point, they then stepped backward and regenerated a model of twenty thousand facets. This model retained the basic qualities of the real landscape and served as the test model for a hologram. They then exported the digital landscape as an .obj file type. Later, they regenerated a more detailed model for the HoloLens that consisted of 270,000 facets, whose topography was an excellent match of the real landscape, greatly surpassing the resolution of a 7.5-minute USGS quad map.

As a side note, if GPS data is embedded in the images or if the user takes time to georeference specific landmarks on the landscape model with latitude, longitude, and elevation data (easily obtained in Google Earth), the object can be exported as a Collada file (Kronos, n.d.). This file type can then be imported into Google Earth, and the 3D landscape model will show up georeferenced in its appropriate geographic space on Google Earth's globe. A librarian could easily build a catalog of georeferenced 3D objects that users have created.

The researchers then employed the Unity Graphics Engine software for creating holograms for the HoloLens (Figure 4.4). This software is one of the main software types used for the creation of graphics for computer games. A specific version of Unity is available for use with the HoloLens, and users can apply for a noncommercial license to learn how to use it. Unity allowed the users to properly place the hologram in 3D space for the user of the HoloLens. The developers of the hologram are able to place the hologram as close to or far from the HoloLens user as desired as the hologram is opened and viewed through the device. Likewise, the object could be placed behind or above the user such that the user would need to look around and turn her or his head to find the object while wearing the headset. Microsoft Visual Studio is also involved with porting the hologram to the HoloLens, so a new developer may want to load these pieces of software at the same time. It is therefore important that libraries strive to have all possible software ready for their users to ensure that equipment is ready to go, especially for novice users.

Visual Studio, in particular, had some background-dependent software that needed to be loaded, and a few other specific computer parameters had to be changed for the program to work. The researchers are currently using Visual Studio 17 for HoloLens projects, which requires Microsoft Windows 10 Professional software. Additionally, the software needs to be configured to its "developer mode" and the BIOS configuration updated to use hypervirtualization. Additional software requirements were recognized by the Visual Studio software as needed during the process or during loading of the first object from the Unity graphics engine.

When the Unity graphics engine is opened, and the desired digital object imported, the developers have the opportunity to organize the viewing scene. It is important to understand that the developer has an overarching view of the scene that shows where there is virtual lighting for the object, either through the virtual sun or a virtual lamp or series of lamps; the location of the viewer or the viewing device, such as the HoloLens; and the digital object. The developer sees all these items from above, but the created digital object may or may not be lined up with what the viewing field of the device (think HoloLens) can see. This is where the developer is setting the stage for the hologram user to experience the object. The developer can create a situation or environment where a holographic object is directly in front of a person or, as in Pokémon GO, the viewer would need to hunt for or seek out the object. The device viewer may need to look for the object in 3D space by having viewers turn their head side to side, up or down, or even requiring viewers to turn 180 degrees to see the object after the file is opened in the HoloLens. By clicking on the camera icon in the Unity software, the developer will open a

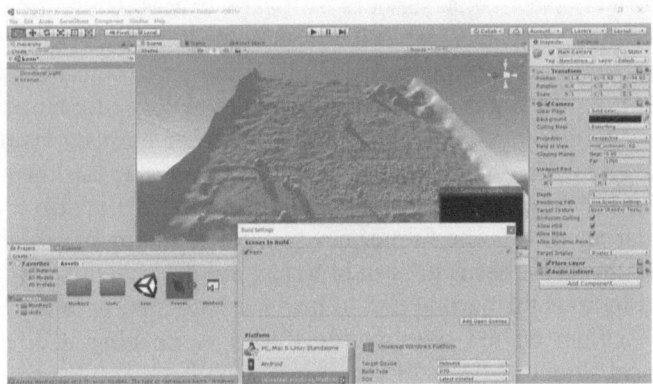

Figure 4.4. Unity Screen. *Photo taken by Dean Walton.*

subwindow that represents what the device user sees, to be sure that the developer positioned the object correctly.

Moving the lighting creates different shadow effects. This is important for landscapes because shadows add to how the brain interprets topographic reliefs. Tweaks to the object's orientation, as seen through the viewing device, should also be done at this point. What looks fine to the developer in the overarching view of the scene may not represent the orientation that the device user will see upon opening the hologram file in the headset. This separation of the developer viewpoint from that of the device user is probably one of the most critical concepts in creating the holograms. The developer must move and turn or otherwise place the object correctly to ensure that the device user can see the object even though the developer can see the object in the developer-viewing window.

In creating the hologram, the HoloLens interprets a black background (RBG 000) as empty space and, thus, this area will be transparent in the HoloLens, allowing the user to see the contents and space around the person and creating the augmented environment. Therefore, to create a hologram that appears to hang locked in position in a nonvirtual room, the researchers selected this choice from Unity's object inspection toolbar. Now, if the digital object is properly placed and oriented in 3D space for the device viewer, the "scene," Unity's term for the object in 3D space, can be exported to a "solution" file type for use by Visual Studio. The "solution" file type is the default file that Unity will create for export.

During this process, users need to select what kind of device should portray the object, such as an Android cell phone versus a HoloLens, and then select Windows 10 Universal SDK as a choice from the Build menu. For the HoloLens, the researchers needed to select the C# program language. No additional programming was needed as C# was just the language used by the system. Since Unity is designed more for video games, its default settings are for that format. New .Net services software causes Unity to default to IL2CPP scripting; however, returning to the object inspector tab and selecting the scripting backend for .Net will allow the user to go back to the C# environment. As the file is developed, the system will ask for a new folder in which to place the developed object solution. After the user creates a new folder and gives the object solution a name, he or she can then open the solution file in Visual Studio. An additional solution file is also created at a higher folder layer. It is the former newly created and more nested solution file that the developer needs to open in Visual Studio.

Visual Studio is the porting tool to load the hologram onto the HoloLens, either by clicking on the solution file (*.sln) or opening it directly from within Visual Studio. Microsoft provides a HoloLens emulator, which is a great way to test the system and see if the HoloLens would show the hologram without error. When users open the solution file, Visual Studio may pause and update itself with any other needed dependent libraries. The emulator system also needs to be installed separately. The system will be downloaded from a Microsoft site as a .msi file that will install itself. Once the installation is complete, users can select the appropriate chip system for the HoloLens. The HoloLens is an X86 chip system. Next, select the target device (HoloLens emulator or HoloLens). As a test, the HoloLens emulator should be selected. The last step is to click "Run without debugging" from the Debug menu. The HoloLens emulator then opens up the hologram.

A person new to the HoloLens will need to learn its basic navigation menus. As the HoloLens emulator opens, a rectangular screen appears in the viewing area of the emulated device. In the emulator, the arrow keys allow the user to move what would be the person's head in the real device to see various sections of areas of the 3D viewing space. However, the main menu screen is right in front of the viewing area. Depending on how many holograms have been added, a user may need to select the next screen or more item tabs from the menu. At some point in this process, an icon tile for the created holograms becomes visible. Again, moving the arrow keys allows the developer to select the right tile icon for the hologram. The emulator should now show the Unity graphics engine opening and then display the hologram.

With the success of the emulator deployment, the researchers were then ready to go back to Visual Studio and change the target device from HoloLens emulator to HoloLens and run the commands again. Visual Studio will ask for a pairing number that will be visible on the HoloLens. Holograms can be deployed via Wi-Fi or via a wired USB connection from the computer to the device. In either case, the HoloLens needs to be opened, and the user will need to navigate to the Utilities pages and set the HoloLens to developer mode. Both ways have worked successfully.

The holograms are now accessible via the Hologram menu on the HoloLens. The navigation process is the same as on the emulator except now a set of hand and eye position cues are used to move a digital selection "dot" to the appropriate desired menu tile. When the user moves the dot to the desired tab or tile icon in the user's viewing area on a digital menu, the dot changes to a ring to indicate that the user can make a selection. A snap of the fingers in the visual field of the device then completes the command. With the hologram open and floating in space in front of the viewer, the hologram can be placed in the real-world space by selecting the placement icon, using finger pinching and finger snapping commands to move the hologram around the room (Figure 4.5).

The development of the process is quite exciting. Having landscapes that a user can zoom in and out of to see a landform at various scales is captivating. One of the more exciting ventures involved deploying a large holographic model of Mount Saint Helens in the library. The model was uploaded by someone else to Thingiverse, a repository of 3D printable objects (Thingi-

Figure 4.5. Wood Hologram. *Photo taken by Dean Walton.*

verse, n.d.). The author and colleagues had previously made 3D prints of this model, but later ported it to the HoloLens. In this situation, researchers scaled it such that it was a three-meter-tall by ten-meter-diameter hologram. Users of the HoloLens could walk around parts of the base of the volcano (some parts digitally extend into the library's walls) or walk up the library's staircase to peer down into the volcano's caldera.

The use of UAVs, SfM, and holograms is a very quick way to make accurate landscape models. One would expect the technology to be useful in emergencies and complex technical situations. In fact, the US Army has now contracted with Microsoft to develop new systems that utilize the power of the HoloLens (Bloomberg.com 2018). At the University of Oregon campus, there is interest in the HoloLens from faculty and/or students in the departments of business, computer science, geology, geography, neuroscience, and physics, and the library is just the place to allow everyone the opportunity to explore this system. While the technology is in its infancy and will rapidly grow, this chapter provides some examples of research use of the HoloLens, walks readers through many of the steps needed to make and utilize holograms, and lets libraries see the technology, equipment, and expertise that is needed to offer a successful HoloLens program.

REFERENCES

Agisoft Photoscan. n.d. Accessed July 11, 2019. http://www.agisoft.com/.

Agten, Christoph, Cyrill Dennler, Andrea B. Rosskopf, Laurenz Jaberg, Christian W. A. Pfirrmann, and Mazda Farshad. 2018. "Augmented Reality-Guided Lumbar Facet Joint Injections." *Investigative Radiology* 53, no. 8: 495–98.

Bloomberg.com. 2018. "Microsoft Wins $480 Million Army Battlefield Contract." *Bloomberg*, November 28, 2018. https://www.bloomberg.com/news/articles/2018-11-28/microsoft-wins-480-million-army-battlefield-contract.

Carmichael, Richie. 2016. "ESRI Holomap." YouTube video. 1:44. December 9, 2016. https://www.youtube.com/watch?v=hE9GXpZTwAs.

Case Western Reserve University. 2015. "CWRU Takes the Stage at Microsoft's Build Conference to Show How HoloLens Can Transform Learning." April 29, 2015. http://case.edu/hololens/.

Cipresso, Pietro, Irene Alice Chicchi Giglioli, Mariano Alcañiz Raya, and Giuseppe Riva. 2018. "The Past, Present, and Future of Virtual and Augmented Reality Research: A Network and Cluster Analysis of the Literature." *Frontiers in Psychology* 9: 2086.

Erat, Okan, Werner Alexander Isop, Denis Kalkofen, and Dieter Schmalstieg. 2018. "Drone-Augmented Human Vision: Exocentric Control for Drones Exploring Hidden Areas." *IEEE Transactions on Visualization and Computer Graphics* 24, no. 4: 1437–46.

Fonstad, Mark A., James T. Dietrich, Brittany C. Courville, Jennifer L. Jensen, and Patrice E. Carbonneau. 2013. "Topographic Structure from Motion: A New Development in Photogrammetric Measurement." *Earth Surface Processes and Landforms* 38, no. 4: 421–30.

Golparvar-Fard, Mani, and Silvio Savarese. 2011. "Monitoring Changes of 3D Building Elements from Unordered Photo Collections." 2011 IEEE International Conference on Computer Vision Workshops (ICCV Workshops). Barcelona, Spain.

Guo, Fu-Sheng, and Wei Gao. 2013. "Batch Reconstruction from UAV Images with Prior Information." *Acta Automatica Sinica* 39, no. 6: 834–45.

von Haxthausen, Felix, Sonja Jaeckle, Christian Schumann, Ivo Kuhlemann, Veronica García-Vázquez, Juljan Bouchagiar, Anna-Catharina Höfer, Florian Matysiak, Gereon Hüttmann, Jan Peter Goltz, Markus Kleemann, Floris Ernst, and Marco Horn. 2018. "Navigation and Visualisation with HoloLens in Endovascular Aortic Repair." *Innovative Surgical Sciences* 3, no. 3: 167–77.

Jang, Jihye, Cory M. Tschabrunn, Michael Barkagan, Elad Anter, Bjoern Menze, and Reza Nezafat. 2018. "Three-Dimensional Holographic Visualization of High-Resolution Myocardial Scar on HoloLens." *PLoS ONE* 13, no. 10: e0205188.

Kawanishi, Ryosuke, Atsushi Yamashita, Toru Kaneko, and Hajime Asama. 2013. "Parallel Line-Based Structure from Motion by Using Omnidirectional Camera in Textureless Scene." *Advanced Robotics* 27, no. 1: 19–32.

Kronos. n.d. *COLLADA*. Accessed July 12, 2019. https://www.khronos.org/collada/.

Martínez-Murilloa, Juan Francisco, Estela Nadal-Romero, David Regüés, Artemi Romina Cerda, and Jean Poesen. 2013. "Soil Erosion and Hydrology of the Western Mediterranean Badlands throughout Rainfall Simulation Experiments: A Review." *Catena* 106: 101–12.

Microsoft. n.d. Microsoft HoloLens. Accessed July 12, 2019. https://www.microsoft.com/en-us/hololens.

Microsoft HoloLens. 2016. "Partners Make It Real." YouTube video. 1:32. March 30, 2016. https://www.youtube.com/watch?v=VzAwdBZ3KCQ.

Milanesi, Pietro, Rolf Holderegger, Kurt Bollmann, Felix Gugerli, and Florian Zellweger. 2017. "Three-Dimensional Habitat Structure and Landscape Genetics: A Step Forward in Estimating Functional Connectivity." *Ecology* 98, no. 2: 393–402.

Moreta-Martinez, Rafael, David García-Mato, Mónica García-Sevilla, Rubén Pérez-Mañanes, José Calvo-Haro, and Javier Pascau. 2018. "Augmented Reality in Computer-Assisted Interventions Based on Patient-Specific 3D Printed Reference." *Healthcare Technology Letters* 5, no. 5: 162–66.

National Futur. 2016. "Microsoft HoloLens Partner Spotlight Greg Lynn." YouTube video. 2:37. June 3, 2016. https://www.youtube.com/watch?v=_njyw192oY8.

Pix4D. n.d. Accessed July 12, 2019. https://www.pix4d.com/.

Siminski, Keenan. 2018. "University of Oregon 3D-Modeling Drone." University of Oregon (blog). November 30, 2018. https://blogs.uoregon.edu/modelingdrone/.

Snavely, Noah, Steven M. Seitz, and Richard Szeliski. 2008. "Modeling the World from Internet Photo Collections." *International Journal of Computer Vision* 80, no. 2: 189–210. https://doi.org/10.1007/s11263-007-0107-3.

Thingiverse. n.d. Accessed July 12, 2019. https://www.thingiverse.com/.
Unity Graphics Engine. n.d. Accessed July 12, 2019. https://unity3d.com/partners/microsoft/mixed-reality.
Visual Studio, Microsoft. n.d. Accessed July 12, 2019. https://visualstudio.microsoft.com/vs/whatsnew/.
Walton, Dean P. 2014, July 12. "Trials and Tribulations of Drones (UAVs) for Ecological Monitoring." Society for Conservation GIS, Monterey, CA.
Walton, Dean P. 2015, May 24. "GIS Incorporation of Structure-from-Motion Models Utilizing Disaster Response Related Imagery." Poster presented at the Information Systems for Crisis Response and Management (ISCRAM) annual meeting, Kristiansand, Norway.
Walton, Dean P., P. Gordon, G. S. Pitts, and S. Proctor. 2017a, July 7–9. "2D and 3D Mapping of the Long Tom River via UAV Systems for Long-Term Change Detection and Conservation – A MOS-OCF Project." Poster presented at the Oregon Country Fair (unpublished).
Walton, Dean P. 2017b, July. "The Painted Hills: Exploration of 3D Visualization and Hologram Generation as Tools for Conservation and Ecological Analysis" Poster presented at the Society for Conservation GIS, Monterey, CA.
Walton, Dean P. 2018, November 16. "From the Ground to the HoloLens." American Society for Photogrammetry and Remote Sensing Conference, University of Oregon.
Wang, Shiyao, Michael Parsons, Jordan Stone-McLean, Peter Rogers, Sarah Boyd, Kristopher Hoover, Oscar Meruvia-Pastor, Minglun Gong, and Andrew Smith. 2017. "Augmented Reality as a Telemedicine Platform for Remote Procedural Training." *Sensors* 17, no. 10: 1–21. https://doi.org/10.3390/s17102294.
Wang, Wei, Xingxing Wu, Guanchen Chen, and Zeqiang Chen. 2018. "Holo3DGIS: Leveraging Microsoft HoloLens in 3D Geographic Information." *ISPRS International Journal of Geo-Information* 7, no. 2: 60. https://doi.org/10.3390/ijgi7020060.
Wiebrands, Michael, Chris J. Malajczuk, Andrew J. Woods, Andrew L. Rohl, and Ricardo L. Mancera. 2018. "Molecular Dynamics Visualization (MDV): Stereoscopic 3D Display of Biomolecular Structure and Interactions Using the Unity Game Engine." *Journal of Integrative Bioinformatics* 15, no. 2: 1–8. https://doi.org/10.1515/jib-2018-0010.
Zmarz, Anna, Mirosław Rodzewicz, Maciej Dąbski, Izabela Karsznia, Małgorzata Korczak-Abshire, and Katarzyna J. Chwedorzewska. 2018. "Application of UAV BVLOS Remote Sensing Data for Multi-Faceted Analysis of Antarctic Ecosystem." *Remote Sensing of Environment* 217 (August): 375–88. https://doi.org/10.1016/j.rse.2018.08.031.

Chapter Five

Creating Ideas into Reality

Spaces and Programs That Open Up the Imagination

Kari Kozak

Virtual reality, 3D scanning, Arduino programming, oh my! The Lichtenberger Engineering Library at the University of Iowa designed a new 575-square-foot area called the Creative Space, a place for students, faculty, and staff to turn their ideas into reality and to get hands-on experience. The room enriches programs and resources already in place within the college, including the engineering electronics shop, engineering machine shop, and the Tool Library. The new resources allow users to explore the latest in virtual reality, 3D scanning and modeling, Arduino programming, and wearable technology.

With the addition of the new space, the toolLibrary, with a wide variety of hand and measuring tools for checkout, has been steadily increasing in size and currently has 225 items available. Between September 2012 and December 2018, 7,256 items were checked out; the most popular were the calculators, twenty-five-foot tape measure, digital caliper, LabQuest testing equipment, screwdriver sets, and the multimeters. Programming, marketing, and word of mouth led to a significant increase in the use of the Tool Library, with 1,703 items checked out during the fall 2018 semester alone.

To enhance the user experience and to assist in offsetting costs to the inventor, the Engineering Technology Center and Lichtenberger Engineering Library teamed up to create a scholarship/grant program called Creative Kick-Start. For the last three years, up to ten groups/individuals were each awarded $500 to be used in either the electronic or machine shop on materials, labor, and tools needed to make their idea a reality within a six-month period.

In addition to the Kick-Start program, the library has hosted a variety of hands-on workshops. These workshops teach students in an engaging way versatile skills that can later be applied to their own projects. A side benefit is an increased awareness and visibility of the Tool Library and space. The hands-on workshops are taught by staff and faculty across campus.

This Creative Space and Kick-Start program stimulate students to imagine, tinker, design, and, ultimately, create new and innovative projects. The Tool Library provides additional resources to bring design projects into being.

BACKGROUND

The Tool Library project began in 2012 with a single email from a professor asking if the Engineering Library would be open to checking out tools. The professor had tools to loan to students but no system for tracking the items. The library was eager to add this new service and set up procedures and a loan policy. (Full policy and procedures can be found at http://www.lib.uiowa.edu/eng/tool-library/.) The Tool Library started out with thirty-eight items available for checkout, and items have been added ever since. News of the new Tool Library spread by word of mouth, triggering several different groups to donate tools.

At the beginning of 2016, it became apparent there was a need for items geared toward creating and hands-on learning with a strong emphasis on technology. Library staff noticed that an outdated classroom and an adjoining storage room could be converted into a more usable space.

The College of Engineering already had the electronic shop and the machine shop in the building, providing 3D printing and other prototyping services, and including a method for collecting payments and staffing for continuous maintenance. Essentially, all the College of Engineering was missing was a place to design and develop these ideas before sending them to production. The idea of a place to create ideas and gain hands-on training from scratch is the origin of the Creative Space.

During the spring of 2016, the head librarian visited several regional university makerspaces to get a feel for what others in the field were undertaking. Three general themes developed from these visits and subsequent discussions:

1. Prototyping (including 3D scanning and printing)
2. Virtual reality
3. Computer programming/circuit building

In the summer of 2016, the Lichtenberger Engineering Library took a small computer classroom and a storage room and turned them into a 575-square-foot makerspace called the Creative Space. The library's newly renovated room includes tinkering stations with access to different technologies, tools, and areas for collaborative work, featuring whiteboards and quad monitors. This room is a place for students, faculty, and staff to turn their ideas into reality and to provide hands-on experience.

The Tool Library, located inside the Engineering Library, was also enhanced. Technology-based items, such as 360 cameras, 3D scanners, Arduino kits, light meters, thermal cameras, and more, were added as complements to the basic measuring tools available. These new resources allow the user to explore the latest in virtual reality, 3D scanning and modeling, Arduino programming, and wearable technology.

By May 2019, there were more than 225 tools in the Tool Library. There have been roughly 100 tools added since 2016, all at the request of students and faculty. These new tools include a speed gun, surveying equipment, oscilloscope, and soldering irons.

DESIGNING THE SPACE

The book *The Engineer of 2020* recognized that creating, inventing, and innovating are essential skills for engineers (National Academy of Engineering 2004). The need for spaces to help foster these skills has led to makerspaces becoming increasingly popular with university libraries. These spaces provide opportunities for students, faculty, and staff to gain hands-on learning; thus, sparking their imaginations and allowing them to be innovative and think outside the box. The library is an ideal setting for these spaces because it allows users from varied disciplines to work together and learn from each other.

When designing the Creative Space within the Lichtenberger Engineering Library, a major emphasis was to ensure the room had a welcoming and comfortable environment. No large equipment intimidating to students is visible when first entering the space (Sparrow 2016). Another major consideration was to ensure ample amounts of versatile seating and tables. The flexible space supports innovation and creativity in relation to two types of learning—exploitation and exploration—and five types of behaviors (Bieraugel and Stern 2017, 36):

1. Observing
2. Questioning
3. Experimenting
4. Networking

5. Reflecting

The configuration generates an adaptable, open, collaborative space to encourage creativity with glass whiteboards, counter-height movable tables, and large computer monitors with multiple laptop connections. Computers along the back wall include numerous software packages needed for creating and designing in a digital environment but do not dominate the room. The equipment is stored out of the way but can be checked out as needed, all helping to create a welcoming atmosphere that encourages users to work through all steps of the creating and innovating process.

THE CREATIVE SPACE AND TOOL LIBRARY

The Creative Space and the Tool Library now feature 225 tools, available for student, faculty, and staff checkout, and a 575-square-foot room complete with the tools and technology necessary to create projects related to prototyping, virtual reality, and programming/circuit building. The space focuses on versatility without assigning what can be done to only one place in the room. This allows for users to manipulate the space as they need. Five whiteboards and two easily movable open tables are features of the room, allowing for exploring, experimenting, and creating projects. Two collaboration tables with 4K quad monitors are perfect for group work, as are computers available for 3D scanning, designing, and modeling. One dedicated computer for use with virtual reality systems requires an equivalent GTX 970/AMD R9 290 video card or greater. A full floor plan is shown in Figure 5.1.

The Tool Library has been steadily growing with continuous requests from students and faculty. Many of the requests come from students who are working on senior design projects or student organizations that need to test their products. One example is the solar car team that needed an oscilloscope to test solar panels. Items that will be added over the summer of 2019 include EEK, EMG, vice grips, surveying equipment, and an HTC Vive. All but the virtual reality sets and cables may be checked out for seven days to use within the Creative Space, in class, or to take home. A complete list of all tools currently available is shown in Appendix A.

All of these tools and other items are only a fraction of the resources available to promote innovation and creation within the Creative Space. The whiteboards and computers and the arrangement within the space allow students the opportunity to brainstorm and explore their ideas. The space and the Tool Library together allow for further exploration of ideas and the opportunity to observe those innovations in action. Since the room is open to all, student interaction, networking, and sharing of concepts and designs are facilitated. Students especially enjoy the interactive items, such as the Oculus

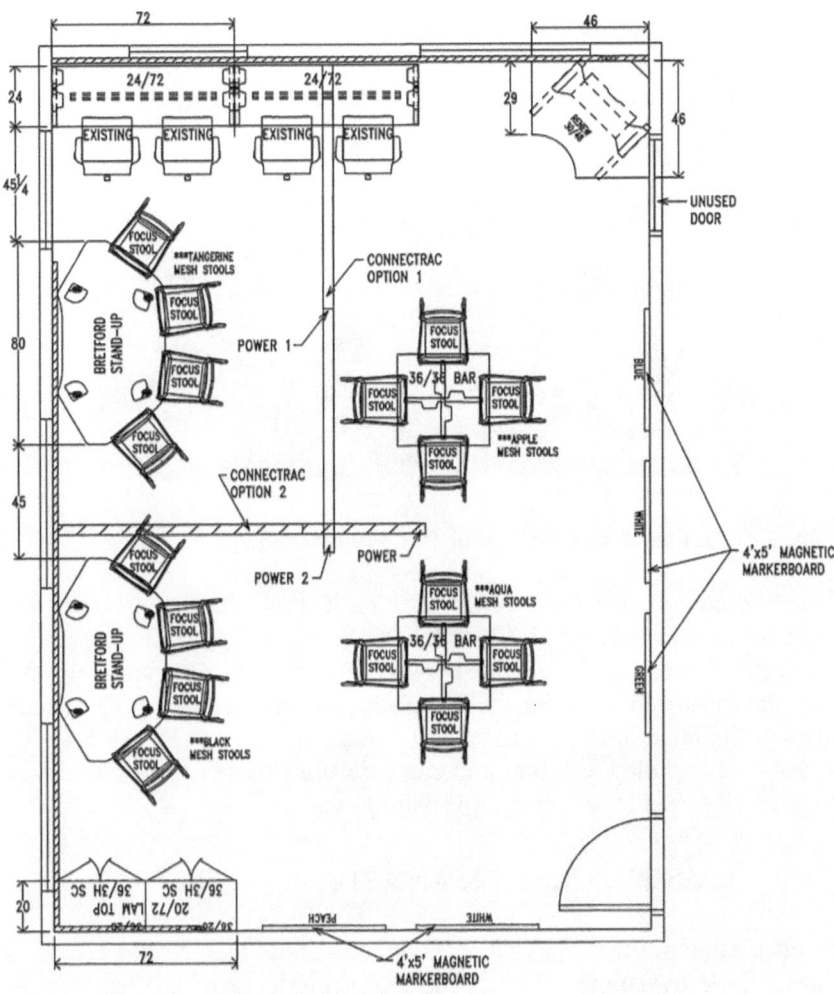

Figure 5.1. Floor Plan of the Creative Space. *Created by Kari Kozak.*

Rift (Figure 5.2), and the collaboration items, including whiteboards and group tables (Figure 5.3).

USE STATISTICS

The addition of the Creative Space and the acquisition of new items in the Tool Library triggered a significant rise in use statistics. This use has been steadily increasing each year as more and more professors tell their students

Figure 5.2. Student Using the Oculus Rift. *Photo taken by Kari Kozak.*

to use the equipment. There have been 7,256 tools checked out since the program began in 2012 and 1,703 in fall 2018.

Of all the items checked out between September 2012 and December 2018, the most popular were the calculator, twenty-five-foot tape measure, ruler set, digital caliper, and LabQuest measuring device (Figure 5.4). This list does not include the cables and chargers since these are for one-day use and not really used for creating or designing.

CLASS INTEGRATION AND STUDENT FEEDBACK

The integration of the Creative Space with classroom projects has been slowly developing over time. Most of the first semester was devoted to giving tours of the space to faculty and speaking about opportunities for collaboration. During the fall 2018 semester, a class on 3D printing used the various types of 3D scanners so the students could test the same object with various scanners and see how it changes the quality of the 3D print. Several engineering classes, as well as a digital art class and a library science class, also brought their students in for a tour.

The equipment and space have been used for individual class projects. An undergraduate student of art designed his honors senior performance project in the virtual reality environment of Oculus Rift. Another student used the 3D scanner to scan different-sized candies in order to model different sizes of cancer tumors to build a database doctors can use to explain tumor sizes to patients. Individual students have found the room very beneficial for their

Figure 5.3. Students Using Whiteboards and Collaborative Tables. *Photo taken by Kari Kozak.*

projects. The following from Jared Becker, a 2017 senior in mechanical engineering, helps to highlight the effectiveness of the space:

> I want to thank you for supporting myself and my peers in our continued pursuit of knowledge and academic excellence here, at the University of Iowa. The Creative Space provides a highly engaging and collaborative atmosphere unlike anywhere else in the Engineering College. Myself and my classmates find that the room's advanced technological access provides a highly stimulating atmosphere necessary for creative problem solving. Also, this space provides a very natural feel: the sleek design, abundant windows and natural lighting provides a sense of comfort and mental clarity when processing complicated problem sets or feeling overwhelmed by course work; we are very grateful for its existence.
>
> Thank you again for helping to enrich my academic experience and I hope you can continue to support my desire to make a change in the world.

The uses for the equipment and space within the Lichtenberger Engineering Library are endless. One of the biggest hurdles for the students was how to pay for the cost of prototyping their ideas. The cost of materials can be a problem for many students. To battle this problem, the Engineering Technology Center and the Lichtenberger Engineering Library teamed up to create the Creative Kick-Start program.

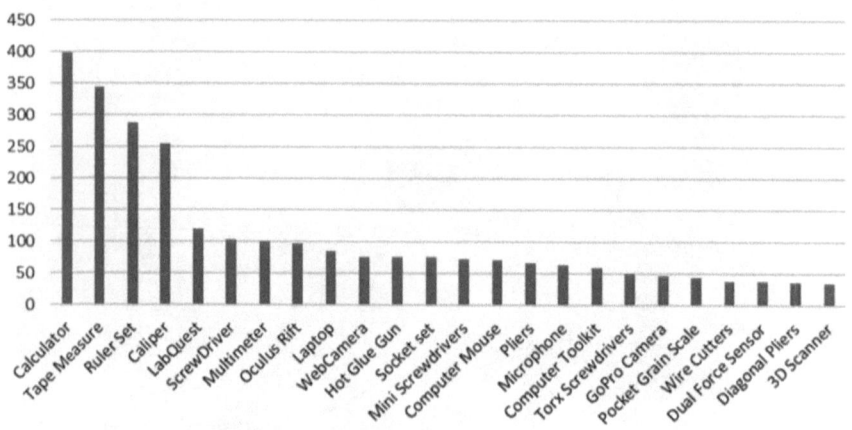

Figure 5.4. Top Twenty-Five Tools Checked Out from Fall 2015 to Fall 2018. *Table created by Kari Kozak.*

OUTREACH

Kick-Start Project

The Creative Space is part of an entire network within the College of Engineering providing services and resources for students to create and build. The Engineering Technology Center, which includes the electronic shop and the machine shop, is part of this network and offers students, faculty, and staff a way to complete their projects, seeing them through the final steps of building and 3D printing. Due to the need for cost recovery of consumable items, there may be some nominal costs for students using the services available through the electronic shop or machine shop. Understanding that these costs might be a barrier to students completing their projects, the Engineering Technology Center put forward $5,000 to create a grant program for students. This program is run through the Lichtenberger Engineering Library.

Using the Adobe Kickbox (Adobe Systems, n.d.) and the Elon University Kickbox programs (Reis, n.d.) as models, the Creative Kick-Start program was developed for engineering students (undergraduate and graduate) to request funding to help pay for prototyping/finishing their projects through the services provided by Creative Space, the engineering electronics shop, and the machine shop. Up to ten awards of $500 each are given out annually since 2017. These awards must be used in the electronics and/or machine shops.

The process for this program includes the following steps:

- Thinking of an idea for a project that can be completed in roughly six months (the first year it was three months, but the last two have been six)
- Identifying a faculty or staff sponsor to offer support and advice
- Completing an online application explaining the idea and why it is worth pursuing
- Attending one of two in-person workshops offered in the fall semester (inventors receive a fund code to access their $500 at the workshop)
- Providing two progress reports midway through the year documenting a meeting between sponsor and inventor
- Presenting their project as a poster during the College of Engineering Research Open House in April
- Providing an expense report at the completion of their project

The library and technology center did not have any specific projects in mind. Students could solve a problem in the world, on campus, or in their room; projects could be a prototype or a finished product. The inventions manager from the Research Foundation, the faculty lead for the Founders Club, a part of the University Entrepreneurial Center, and representatives from the machine shop and the electronic shop attended to provide additional information to the students about patenting and the possibilities of creating businesses from their projects.

All the award winners are asked if they are planning to patent their idea or project. This question requires the library to alter what information will be sent out for marketing. The descriptions sent out to the general public had to be vague enough not to violate the public disclosure agreement before beginning the patent process.

In April, each student will present his or her poster at the College of Engineering Research Open House. During this event, participants showcase their projects and discuss how they have evolved throughout the semester. The students have been told from the start that it is okay if the projects fail since failure is merely a stepping-stone in the innovation process. Even if the project "fails," the presentation is still mandatory. In addition to presenting at the open house, the students may also volunteer to present their projects during the campus-wide Innovation Expo at the end of April.

Some of the projects that have been completed over the last three years include The Little Jonny That Could: Providing Independence for Congenital Arm Amputees, Precision Landing System for Autonomous Aircraft, Smart Mirror, The KnowGlobe, Convert Any Piano to a Player Piano, Body Betty, Air Chair, and Metered Dose Sunscreen Device. A list of the seven projects that completed the Creative Kick-Start program in 2018–2019, along with a summary of their presentations including lessons learned and challenges, is provided in Appendix B.

Participants in the Creative Kick-Start program have filled out surveys that indicate an average rating of 4.5 out of 5 for being satisfied with the program. One student participant in 2018 said, "The kick start program was a great thing for me this past year. Not only did I get to know the materials available to engineering students, but I got to work on a project that I never would have been able to in my discipline." A faculty sponsor from 2018 stated, "While the actual dollar amount is small, it is more than enough to excite the students into thinking they can build a real item. BME design teams supported by the Kickstart program have more design iterations and more testing compared to teams that don't. This is a very valuable catalyst that drives the team forward in their design process."

The Creative Kick-Start project provides a great opportunity for students to work through the entire process—developing a project, writing a proposal, working under a deadline, and presenting their work. In addition to providing a unique opportunity for students, the program has the added benefit of marketing the Creative Space, electronic shop, and machine shop to those within the college and the campus as a whole.

Learn and Create Workshops

Since spring 2018, the library has worked together with various staff and faculty around campus to create hands-on workshops. These workshops provide students, faculty, and staff from across campus an opportunity to use the equipment and tools inside the library, learn new skills, create, and innovate. Some of the more popular workshops include soldering basics taught by an engineering staff member, creating pop-cards taught by the director of art and engineering, and making a capacitive touch mini-piano cotaught by a staff member in engineering and a faculty member in music. Thus far, twenty-eight workshops were offered with 222 participants attending. The average is about eight participants per workshop. Given the small space and to ensure the hands-on experience, there is a cap of twenty-five students in a session. The average rating for the workshops is 4.3 out of 5 for being useful.

Bringing the workshops to the library allows students, faculty, and staff to learn about the Creative Space and Tool Library, and it also provides a great opportunity for learning and exchanging ideas. The students have a chance to learn about areas they may not see otherwise. For example, several of the students in the soldering workshop were civil engineering students who wouldn't have had the chance to learn to solder otherwise, as soldering is only taught in electrical and computer engineering classes.

The workshops and the Creative Kick-Start program provide another effective marketing venue. These programs allow the students to begin to explore the possibilities of what they can do in the space by themselves. Over the last three years, some innovative projects have been completed, and it will be exciting to see what the future brings.

CONCLUSION

"Creativity, invention, and innovation are values championed as central pillars of engineering education" (Forest et al. 2014, 1). The Creative Space and the Tool Library work to encompass all aspects of creation and innovation learning and behaviors: exploiting, exploring, observing, questioning, experimenting, networking, and reflecting. The space, equipment, and programming allow the students to open up their imagination and work to make their ideas a reality. The collaboration between the Engineering Technology Center and the Creative Space enhances services offered by both entities to ensure that students can fully explore all aspects of innovation by providing opportunities to tinker, explore, brainstorm, and create.

ACKNOWLEDGMENTS

Thank you to the Engineering Technology Center for all their support through this whole process, including John Kostman, Matt McLaughlin, Tom Barnhart, Doug Eltoft, Christopher Fomon, Daniel Mentzer, and Danny Tang. Lichtenberger Engineering Library staff (James Cox, Carol Johnk, and Qianjin Marina Zhang) are vital to the programs' and resources' success.

Thank you to all those at the University of Minnesota (Liberal Arts Technologies and Innovation Services), Medical Device Center, Walter Engineering Library, and DigiFabLab [College of Design]), University of Wisconsin–Madison (Wendt Commons [Engineering Library], Garage Physics, and Discovery Building), and University of Illinois–Urbana-Champaign (Undergraduate Library and Granger Engineering Library) for meeting to share your experiences and ideas.

REFERENCES

Adobe Systems. n.d. "Adobe KickBox." Accessed October 9, 2019. https://kickbox.org.
Bieraugel, Mark, and Stern Neill. 2017. "Ascending Bloom's Pyramid: Fostering Student Creativity and Innovation in Academic Library Spaces." *College & Research Libraries* 78, no. 1: 35–53.
Forest, Craig. R., Roxanne A. Moore, Amit S. Jariwala, Barbara Burks Fasse, Julie Linsey, Wendy Newstetter, Peter Ngo, and Christopher Quintero. 2014. "The Invention Studio: A University Maker Space and Culture." *Advances in Engineering Education* 4, no. 2. http://advances.asee.org/publication/the-invention-studio-a-university-maker-space-and-culture/.
Kozak, Kari A. 2017. "Creating Ideas into Reality: Spaces and Programs That Open Up the Imagination." Conference Proceedings T421A: Technical Session: The History & Future of

Engineering Librarianship. *American Society of Engineering Education Annual Conference*, Columbus, OH, June 2017.

National Academy of Engineering. 2004. *The Engineer of 2020: Visions of Engineering in the New Century*. Washington, DC: National Academies Press.

Reis, D. n.d. "Makers Hub: Elon Kickbox." Elon University. https://www.elon.edu/e/org/makers/kickbox/index.html.

Sparrow, J. 2016. "Featured Speaker: 21st-Century Digital Citizenship." Presentation at 4Cast Conference, Iowa City, IA, January 12, 2016. https://4cast.uiowa.edu/schedule.

APPENDIX A: FULL LIST OF AVAILABLE TOOLS

LIST OF AVAILABLE TOOLS

The Tool Library offers a wide variety of tools from hand tools to measuring tools and everything in between! And more tools are being added regularly!

3D Scanners: Sense 3D Scanner, Structure Sensor for iPad scanner, Xbox Kinnect

Cameras: 360Fly 4k camera, Canon Powershot, GoPro Hero 5, RICOH Theta S, sports camcorder, Theta S 360-Degree camera, thermal camera, and an Eyeball Webcam

Computer & Phone Accessories: acoustic microphone, Wacom Drawing Tablets, 2 projectors, wireless presenter, Eyeball Webcam, conference camera system, various chargers and adapters

Hand Tools: Various wrenches, claw hammer, heat gun kit, Hex-Keys, hot glue gun, pliers sets, wide variety of screwdrivers, sheet metal hole punch, socket set, soldering iron, and much more

LabQuest: LabQuest Data Collector, 3-Axis Accelerometer, CO_2 sensor, dual-range force sensor, EKG sensor, electrode amplifier, low-g accelerometer, magnetic field sensor, sound level meter, stainless steel temperature probe, thermocouple, Watts Up Pro, wireless dynamic sensor system, salinity sensor

Laptops & Tablets: 6 Lenovo ThinkPad Laptops and 12 iPads

Measuring Tools: caliper, digital scale, environmental meter, infrared thermometer, laser distance measurer, level & magnetic angle locator, light meter, micrometer, multimeter (volt meter), oscilloscope, pocket grain weight scale, power monitor, speed gun, sound level meter, tachometer, tape measure, triple beam balance, tubular spring scales, vibration meter, wireless temperature probe

Programming & Circuits: MaKey MaKey kit, Raspberry Pi with Vernier Interface Shield, LittleBits, Inventor's Kit, wearable tech (LilyPad), RedBot Inventor's Kit

Virtual & Augmented Reality: Oculus Rift & Oculus Rift Touch (two-hour checkout), Moverio (two-hour checkout), Leap Motion controllers
Specialty Tools: calculator, ruler set, whiteboard markers

APPENDIX B: 2018–2019 CREATIVE KICK-START WINNERS

COMPILED BY JAMES COX

Air Chair

This group has developed a collapsible crate to protect wheelchairs during flights. It would be marketed to airlines—as airlines are the ones damaging the wheelchairs. Following the conclusion of the flight, the crate would be stored for the next passenger. They have developed a hinge that is 3D printed because the hinges that are (1) commercially available and (2) fit the budget of the project were too weak to meet their needs. A big thing they kept coming back to was this idea of going into a project with a budget in mind. They could design and dream up this incredible device, but their resources weren't unlimited, so the project required a good deal of research into how things could be done but kept at a reasonable price point.

Next Step: 3D printing the hinges and building their final prototype for their senior design project presentation.

Skills Learned: Managing resources and matching ideas to available materials/funds, testing, manufacturing processes required.

Challenges: Money, testing. Wheelchairs are expensive to buy in order to test various ones and to make a prototype crate big enough to hold a wheelchair. Students had to make a smaller box and smaller wheelchair to run the test.

Asonus Tech

This group was developing a device to help those with hearing impairments to detect alarms and alerts. The device has evolved into a smart watch app rather than a stand-alone product. The app can detect loud noises. Currently the app can be set to recognize some sounds (i.e., doorbell if users are sitting in their house watching TV versus fire alarm if users are at work), but due to limitations of available sound databases and computer processing power, when performing analysis of sounds the app creates some false positives.

Next Steps: Continue to refine the app to add more sound level sensitivity options and collect sound samples to increase accuracy of recognizing sounds. Eventually make the app available on the Google Play Store as an alpha testing product.

Skills Learned: Coding, soldering, using a 3D printer.

Challenges: During the learning process of these new skills there are natural hurdles (e.g., debugging code, issues of 3D printing techniques).

Body Betty

The students developed a web app and baby doll to assist in teaching human anatomy to young children with the goal of shrinking the gender gap in STEM fields. The app is currently stored as an executable HTML file. The Kick-Start funds were used to purchase the sensors and hardware that was to power the baby doll. The idea was to use Raspberry Pi to house an RFID receiver, a screen to display the app, and an RFID tag to "answer" the question by tapping the various parts of the baby doll. However, there are too few pins on the Raspberry Pi to accommodate the screen and RFID receiver, so the doll was theoretical. The HTML page worked perfectly.

Next Steps: The students are interested in continuing to refine the product. An Arduino board has enough pins, so the students would like to explore that as a Raspberry Pi replacement.

Skills Learned: Electric circuits, programming (neither student has a background in circuits or programming), RFID technology.

Challenges: They had an idea and were passionate about doing it, but they underestimated how much time it would take to learn all these new skills. So, they gained an appreciation for the process of learning those skills.

Car Turbo Jet Engine

The students modified a car turbo to explore the science behind a jet engine. They got it to work for a few seconds at a time using compressed air; however, after the compressed air was removed, the engine failed to intake enough air to continue the reaction. The students used a good deal of math and previous models to duplicate the engine effect.

Next Steps: The students will probably not be moving forward with this project as parts are expensive and safety is a concern due to welding and human error.

Skills Learned: How to modify a car turbo and properties of propane gas.

Challenges: Parts are expensive, so if something messed up it was difficult to replace. The tools they owned limited what they could do because the system had to be sealed and their welder was on the low end for the size they were looking to do.

Kineta Safety Device

The student wished to create a device that would provide safety and send for help if needed. The device is currently in the circuit and breadboard phase. The student created code to interface with an Arduino mini to communicate with a GPS transmitter, piezo buzzer to alert those around the wearer, and the computer to populate location. The student has enjoyed this project and learning about the hardware design process so much it has caused her to change her major to electrical and computer engineering, and she wants to focus on the hardware side of things.

Next Steps: As the student takes more classes and gains knowledge, it is hoped that the hardware can be made into a smaller, more user-friendly device and a more polished final product. Also, the student is interested in discussing with emergency responders what would be required to have them respond (similar to the Life Alert product).

Skills Learned: Coding, breadboarding, and circuitry.

Challenges: Design process (transforming from an electrical shocking glove to a GPS locating device), learning about liability and weapons on campus, prototyping issues—working with the Arduino mini and the other parts arriving with different connectors and learning how to modify what was received to make them work together.

Optimus Prone

The group is looking to create a shoulder rehabilitation table to accommodate people of various body sizes. They spoke about how there are several exercises that therapists do for the shoulder. However, each therapist has his or her own method, so the group's hope was that this table would standardize these exercises. They finished the design phase and actually ordered $600 of aluminum this morning and will construct it for their final presentation in a few weeks. People have different arm lengths; consequently, the team spent a good part of the year trying to develop a way to raise and lower the table. All the methods they came up with would be too expensive. Fortunately, someone had donated an old dentist chair to one of the labs, and they were able to deconstruct that and use the raising and lowering mechanism in their device.

Next Step: Constructing their table when the aluminum arrives for their senior design presentation.

Skills Learned: Testing designs and protocols. It took them a long time to develop these tests that ultimately took five to ten minutes to complete.

Challenges: Money was a limiting factor in their design project. The students had a good idea but recognized that it was not a feasible option, so they developed a suitable alternative.

Root Canal Pal

Some people are unresponsive to the anesthetic used during dental procedures, which can lead to overdosing (which is expensive for the patient) or pain. Their idea is based on the Buzzy (https://buzzyhelps.com/), which uses vibrations to override the needle pain further down the nerve system. They are looking to stimulate the nerve where the nerves found in the jaw connect to override the pain during dental procedures. They have developed a skin, fat, and bone analog to test the vibration that comes through the jaw (what the vibration pen was used for) and created a housing for the vibration device that attaches to the safety glasses already in use by dentists. At the time of the poster session, their final prototype and half their group was in the College of Dentistry working with faculty members to test its usability and collect their thoughts on it.

Next Step: Their plan was to finish their conversations with the faculty today and make any recommended adjustments to their design. Clinic testing is beyond the scope of their senior design project.

Skills Learned: Pain propagation around the mouth and how to measure vibration.

Challenges: Being that this device is intended for use in a medical office, it had to be designed so that it could be made sterile for future patients; this was the main impetus behind most of their design iterations. Additionally, they spent about a month trying to figure out how to measure vibration.

Chapter Six

Planning, Implementing, and Sustaining Audiovisual Edit Suites as a Learning, Teaching, and Research Resource in an Academic Library

Marc Stoeckle and Christie Hurrell

The Taylor Family Digital Library (TFDL) is the central library at the University of Calgary, a research-intensive university located in Alberta, Canada. The library opened in 2011 and was designed to support technology-enriched learning and research, with spaces such as a data visualization studio, a video creation space, a virtual reality studio, and a makerspace either being purpose built in the original construction or added as user needs changed. Four audiovisual (A/V) edit suites were part of the TFDL's original complement of student-oriented spaces. However, by 2017, the A/V suites were in need of updates: the equipment was out of date and damaged, and it didn't meet the current research and learning needs of the university community. This chapter describes a collaborative effort between the TFDL's technology unit and a music subject specialist librarian to assess, update, operationalize, and evaluate these A/V edit suites.

To accomplish this task, it was crucial to develop a project plan that entailed the necessary steps to reach the most successful outcome. This chapter outlines the four steps undertaken as part of this project: assessing current technology, updating and operationalizing the A/V edit suites, performing initial outreach and programming, and reassessing. The project began in spring 2017 and is ongoing.

ASSESSING CURRENT TECHNOLOGY

The literature on audiovisual production and editing spaces in academic libraries revealed that while a number of academic libraries have included these types of technologically enhanced facilities in either existing or new library buildings (Mandel 2016; Brown et al., 2014), there is relatively little literature that provides specific recommendations on how to implement or assess these initiatives. One exception to this is Mestre and Kurt (2015), who provide several recommendations for renovating existing library spaces to accommodate both video and audio studios based on their experience at the University of Illinois. The current project benefited from purpose-built, sound-resistant rooms; however, the assessment revealed that the original software and hardware setup was not adequate for user needs.

The four A/V edit suites have been available since the TFDL opened in 2011. All four edit suites had a basic configuration, consisting of a studio desk, PC or Mac computers, monitors, basic reference speakers, two MIDI keyboards, and editing software available for students, faculty, and community to use. When a new librarian with responsibilities for music was hired in 2016, one of his first priorities was to assess the suites against the needs of current students and faculty.

The assessment revealed several considerable shortcomings in the current configuration of the suites. Unfortunately, soon after the edit suites were made available to the campus community, users pushed in the speakers' woofers, resulting in a constant crackling sound in three of the four suites. Two of the four rooms were equipped with MIDI keyboards, which were supposed to be used in conjunction with the computers and their installed software. However, a too-short connection cable prevented users from plugging the MIDI keyboard into the computers. Additionally, the MIDI keyboards did not provide a sufficient standard to work on projects at a university level. Two of the edit rooms were equipped with Dell Windows PCs that were not capable of producing higher-end audiovisual products due to the lack of processing speed. Additionally, microphones were not permanently installed into any of the suites. Instead, users utilized USB microphones borrowed from the library and connected these, as well as other peripherals, directly into the PCs, leading to a rapid decay of the hardware. The Mac Pro computers installed in the other two edit rooms were still in good technical condition, having been more recently purchased and having a longer life than the Dell PCs, and supported professional-level audio/video editing software. The furniture was still in good condition although not in line with the small footprint (6.85 m²) of the suites.

The use of the suites was also assessed. When users book the suites using the library's online booking tool, they are asked to indicate how they will use the space. The analysis showed that the most common use was for music production, followed by audio production (Figure 6.1). This evidence helped provide guidance for the type of hardware and software to include in the suites.

The assessment revealed that the A/V edit suites did not meet current research and teaching needs across the institution. Since the goal of the suites is to support A/V editing and recording for students and faculty of all disciplines, the rooms had to be newly equipped to meet the needs of a broad spectrum of users, from amateurs creating basic media to high-level users producing professional-level audio and video products. The goal was to create a space that is suitable for users with almost no experience in audiovisual creation and for users with a more advanced skill set.

UPDATING AND OPERATIONALIZING A/V EDIT SUITES

The initial assessment of the old edit suites revealed that the updated suites needed a specific focus on recording and editing in an interdisciplinary context. Based on an understanding of suite use across the disciplines, the rooms were outfitted to serve slightly different purposes: two of the four rooms would focus on *creating* audiovisual media, and two rooms would focus on *editing* audiovisual media. The selection of hardware and software had to meet two key goals: (1) that the suites would support users with both basic and advanced skill sets and (2) that the suites would support the production and editing of a variety of media formats, including oral history interviews, film and music recording, music production, podcast development, vlogs, voice-overs, and more. The audiovisual material can then be edited, mixed, mastered, and finalized for use in assignments, research projects, websites, theater plays, conference presentations, and so forth. As such, the newly equipped edit suites would create a place in the library for students and

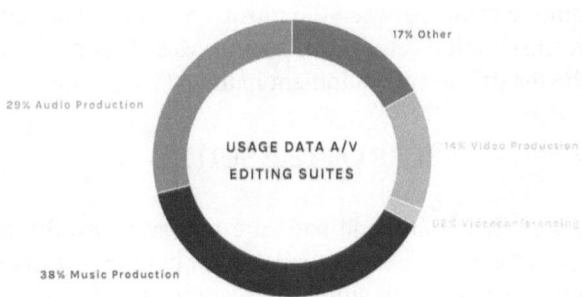

Figure 6.1. Use of A/V Editing Suites, July 2016 to June 2017. *Table created by Marc Stoeckle.*

faculty across all disciplines to work professionally on audiovisual material to meet their research and learning needs.

The two Mac Pro computers and several office chairs were the only equipment reused from the former edit suites. Two additional Mac Pro computers were purchased so that all rooms featured the same computers. In addition to the computers, the renovated suites each contain newly purchased MIDI keyboards for predominantly creating music, basic MIDI and mixing controllers, and, for advanced users, hardware compressors and microphone preamplifiers. The most crucial new purchases for each room were the audio interfaces, which connect all the equipment installed in the A/V edit suites to the computers and function as a translator from analog to digital. The suites with a focus on creating audiovisual media were equipped with the MIDI keyboards (Figure 6.2), and the suites with a focus on editing audiovisual media were equipped with permanently installed microphones and microphone preamplifiers for an improved recording quality (Figure 6.3). The only crucial software purchase that had to be made was a user-friendly, but also professional and industry-leading, audio editing software. In collaboration, the decision was made to purchase four licenses for the audio editing software Logic Pro X, as it is easy to use for new and less experienced users but also meets the needs of professional and high-demand users.

New, smaller studio desks were purchased to make more efficient use of the small space. These desks incorporate the technology more efficiently, creating more space and ensuring that most cables are plugged into inaccessible areas of the furniture, thereby deterring users from modifying the hardware setup in potentially damaging ways. Additionally, microphones and MIDI keyboards were installed permanently to overcome the need for users to plug in equipment on their own.

Although the new hardware and furniture was assessed and recommended by the music librarian, it was purchased from the TFDL's main technology budget. This represented a notable collaboration between two different units in the library to accomplish a shared goal. Installation of the equipment was also a collaborative effort between the music specialist, who has expertise in A/V hardware installation, and the library's Mac desktop specialist. Table 6.1 presents the list of current equipment in the A/V edit suites.

USE OF THE SUITES

Once the furniture, hardware, and software was successfully installed in all four suites, a plan for making them available for booking by library users was developed. While the A/V edit suites are open to students, staff, and faculty at the university, access to them is mediated by a team of student staff members. Bookings are made via the library's online booking system, and

Figure 6.2. Audiovisual Edit Suite for Creating Audiovisual Media. *Photo taken by Marc Stoeckle.*

users must present a campus identification card to access the locked rooms. The default booking limits for the rooms are set to 120 minutes per reservation, two reservations per week. Bookings outside of this limit can be dis-

Figure 6.3. Audiovisual Edit Suite for Editing Audiovisual Media. *Photo taken by Marc Stoeckle.*

cussed with library staff. Because of the size and purpose of the rooms, the capacity is two people, and no food or drink are allowed.

As mentioned previously, the original equipment in the suites had been damaged by users. With the installation of new equipment and software, staff wanted to ensure that the equipment would be well cared for and that novice users would be able to use the more complex software easily. As the team primarily responsible for providing access to and troubleshooting the suites did not have expertise in using the hardware and software, basic training for the student staff team and technology support staff had to be provided as well.

Several new procedures were implemented to address the above concerns:

- Check-in forms: Simple check-in forms were implemented that require a staff member to confirm the condition of each piece of equipment with users at the beginning of their booking. Both the staff member and the user sign off on the form so that there is a paper trail should any damage occur to the rooms or to the equipment.

Table 6.1. Current Equipment in A/V Edit Suites

Category	Creating Suite 1	Creating Suite 2	Editing Suite 1	Editing Suite 2
Computer	*Mac Pro 6-Core (3.5 GHz 6-Core, 16 GB 1866 MHz DDR3 ECC)*	*Mac Pro 6-Core (3.5 GHz 6-Core, 16 GB 1866 MHz DDR3 ECC)*	Mac Pro 6-Core (3.5 GHz 6-Core, 16 GB 1866 MHz DDR3 ECC)	Mac Pro 6-Core (3.5 GHz 6-Core, 16 GB 1866 MHz DDR3 ECC)
Computer Equipment	*Apple Mouse, Apple Keyboard*	*Apple Mouse, Apple Keyboard*	Apple Mouse, Apple Keyboard	Apple Mouse, Apple Keyboard
Displays	*1 X Standard Dell*	*1 X Standard Dell*	1 X Apple Display	1 X Apple Display
Monitors	*2 X Yamaha 6.5-inch Powered Studio Reference Monitor*	*2 X Yamaha 6.5-inch Powered Studio Reference Monitor*	2 X Yamaha 6.5-inch Powered Studio Reference Monitor	2 X Yamaha 6.5-inch Powered Studio Reference Monitor
Audiovisual Software	Logic Pro X, Pro Tools, Audacity, Adobe Creative Suite 5, Final Cut Express, Premier Pro, IMovie, GarageBand	Logic Pro X, Pro Tools, Audacity, Adobe Creative Suite 5, Final Cut Express, Premier Pro, IMovie, GarageBand	Logic Pro X, Pro Tools, Audacity, Adobe Creative Suite 5, Final Cut Express, Premier Pro, IMovie, GarageBand	Logic Pro X, Pro Tools, Audacity, Adobe Creative Suite 5, Final Cut Express, Premier Pro, IMovie, GarageBand
Furniture	2 X Chairs, 1 X Studio Desk Sound Construction DS-KS MP - Maple Finish	2 X Chairs, 1 X Studio Desk Sound Construction DS-KS MP - Maple Finish	2 X Chairs, 1 X Studio Desk Sound Construction DS-KS MP - Maple Finish	2 X Chairs, 1 X Studio Desk Sound Construction DS-KS MP - Maple Finish

Category	Creating Suite 1	Creating Suite 2	Editing Suite 1	Editing Suite 2
Audiovisual Hardware	*Focusrite Scarlett 18i20 USB 2.0 Audio Interface, ART Pro Audio Channel Vactrol/ Tube Leveler Compressor, Arturia 61 Note Keyboard Controller, Korg nanoKONTROL Studio Mobile MIDI Controller*	*Focusrite Scarlett 18i20 USB 2.0 Audio Interface, ART Pro Studio Professional Studio Mic Preamp II, ART Pro Audio Channel Vactrol/ Tube Leveler Compressor, Sennheiser MK4 Condenser Microphone, MKS4 Suspension Mount, Apex 6-inch Dual Screen Nylon Pop Filter, Yorkville Sound Tripod Mic Stand*	*Focusrite Scarlett 18i20 USB 2.0 Audio Interface, ART Pro Audio Channel Vactrol/Tube Leveler Compressor, Arturia 61 Note Keyboard Controller, Korg nanoKONTRO L Studio Mobile MIDI Controller*	*Focusrite Scarlett 18i20 USB 2.0 Audio Interface, ART Pro Studio Professional Studio Mic Preamp II, ART Pro Audio Channel Vactrol/Tube Leveler Compressor, Sennheiser MK4 Condenser Microphone, MKS4 Suspension Mount, Apex 6-inch Dual Screen Nylon Pop Filter, Yorkville Sound Tripod Mic Stand*

Italics - New; Regular text - Original

- Desktop wallpaper: A desktop wallpaper was developed to provide a quick guide for novice users on how to launch A/V editing software and start recording audio. The wallpaper is a convenient, permanent, and highly visible way to provide basic training to users of the suites (Figure 6.4).
- Staff training: Before the newly renovated A/V suites were opened, training was provided to the technology team, including the student staff who mediate access to the suites and to the permanent library staff members who provide ongoing technical support to the suites. This has helped develop protocols for basic troubleshooting as well as in developing relationships between the subject expert and the technology staff. In the latest round of hiring of student staff, the library sought out a student with expertise in A/V recording and editing from the music department. This has increased our capacity to troubleshoot the rooms as well.

Planning, Implementing, and Sustaining Audiovisual Edit Suites 75

OUTREACH AND PROGRAMMING

In order to increase awareness about the updated suites, library staff engaged in a number of outreach and programming activities:

- A research guide was created for the library's website. The guide explains how to book, access, and use the A/V edit suites and provides links to both licensed and free resources for digital image, audio, and video files.
- Outreach was provided within the library so that liaison librarians could promote the suites to their subject areas as appropriate as well as provide outreach to other academic departments whose research and teaching interests align most closely with audiovisual production, such as the music department, and language departments who use the suites for oral history interview recordings or other needs.
- Open library workshops on both music production and general audio production were provided. These workshops respond to library users' professed use of the space and library staff members' observation that many users of the A/V edit suites were not using the hardware and software to their fullest potential. The workshops give learners skills to record, edit, and export music or audio files using Logic Pro. The sessions are team taught by the music librarian and a student worker with expertise in digital audio production and editing.

Library staff members have collaborated with a range of faculty, staff, and students on audiovisual projects. Some examples include the following:

- Collaboration with a special collections librarian, an English professor, and an undergraduate English class to edit field recordings of poetry and

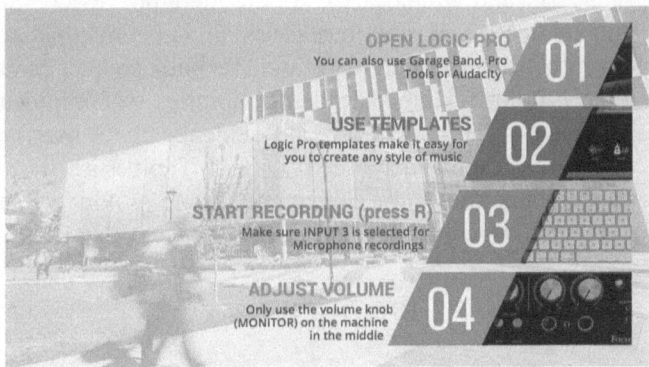

Figure 6.4. Desktop Wallpaper. *Photo taken by Marc Stoeckle.*

fiction readings recorded in a local bookstore for ingestion into the library's special collections
- Assistance for a nursing class developing an educational podcast about cesarean section births
- Training sessions, delivered by a student staff member, for science students engaged in developing a public science engagement video series
- Collaboration with students and professors on oral history interviews, audiovisual assignments, or teaching resources such as instructional videos. As an example, students were asked to create a film for a class assignment, and support was provided to use the A/V suites to record their voices, edit the film, put music and sound effects to the film, and so forth. Other services that are provided are supported with podcasts recorded by students and published on Spotify or music production help for a poetry slam/dance performance.

Since the renovation, operationalization, and promotion of the A/V edit suites, there has been an increase in their use. The suites were occupied 7 percent of the time in 2017, with an increase to 19 percent of the time in 2018. The number of unique users over this period increased by 45 percent (439 from 243), while the total number of bookings increased by 62 percent (1,103 from 419). Average booking duration increased from ninety-one minutes to ninety-eight minutes.

CONCLUSION

This chapter outlines the four steps undertaken as part of this project: assessing current technology, updating and operationalizing the A/V edit suites, providing initial outreach and programming, and reassessing. As noted above, the TFDL assessed, updated, and implemented its A/V editing suites between spring 2017 and winter 2018. As the literature review did not provide substantial evidence of previous cases in implementing audiovisual technology resources in an academic library, this book chapter can be seen as a useful reference point for other academic libraries wishing to implement these types of spaces. The knowledge and evidence about user needs gathered prior to the renovation, combined with staff expertise in audiovisual hardware and software, allows the chapter authors to provide valuable infrastructure for research, teaching, and learning for academic staff and students.

REFERENCES

Brown, Sherri, Charlie Bennett, Bruce Henson, and Alison Valk. 2014. "Next-Gen Learning Spaces." *SPEC Kit 342*. Washington, DC: Association of Research Libraries.

Mandel, Debra. 2016. "Northeastern University Libraries' Digital Media Commons Delivers Creative and Curricular Services to All." *Against the Grain* 28, no. 5: 32, 34.

Mestre, Lori S., and Eric Kurt. 2015. "Excuse Me. Is That a Video Studio in Your Library?" *Re-think It: Libraries for a New Age Conference Proceedings*. ScholarWorks@GVSU. 1-22.

Chapter Seven

A Tale of Two Initiatives

Developing Operational Models for 3D Printing and a Multimedia Production Studio in a STEM Library

Renaine Julian, Kelly Grove, Joshua Julien, and Michael Meth

This chapter provides insight into the challenges and opportunities associated with two technology-related initiatives at the Dirac Science Library at Florida State University (FSU). The first section documents the process associated with assuming responsibility of a multimedia production studio located in the Dirac Science Library, while the second part of the chapter describes the process of creating a mediated 3D printing program for the campus based out of the science library. Both initiatives required developing service models while leveraging existing staff. Establishing these new services created an opportunity for FSU libraries to further support and enhance research and learning activities in the university by providing two important services for the FSU community. These projects created professional development and learning experiences for library staff, who were pivotal in developing and operating these new services.

FSU is located in the city of Tallahassee, the capital of Florida. It is a Research 1 university according to the Carnegie Classification of Institutions of Higher Education and has approximately 42,000 students and over 1,900 members of the faculty. The Paul A. M. Dirac Science Library ("Dirac") was built in 1985 and is located on the west end of FSU's campus. It was renovated in 2012, providing a new café and modernizing the library.

The purpose of this chapter is to allow other libraries to learn and grow from these experiences by sharing the story. While both initiatives had shared and individual challenges, they were worthwhile endeavors that strengthened the libraries' ability to meet student and faculty needs. With the acquisition of the multimedia production studio, the primary challenge was finding ways to assume responsibility for the operation of a new service point while being mindful of its history. The development of a new 3D printing service required developing a complex workflow that contained multiple steps and had to scale quickly to accommodate the rapidly growing demand.

GEOSET MULTIMEDIA PRODUCTION STUDIO

The GEOSET multimedia production studio opened in September 2014 in Dirac after having previously been established as a project by Nobel laureate and FSU faculty member Sir Harry Kroto in FSU's chemistry department. The establishment of the permanent studio in Dirac was the latest addition to the Global Educational Outreach for Science Engineering and Technology (GEOSET) initiative and joined a network of affiliated studios around the world. GEOSET was conceived as a service to leverage the power of video as an educational tool and for scientific knowledge dissemination. The service was designed to allow the university community, particularly students and faculty, to record short videos to showcase their work.

During the fall of 2016, the university administration approached the libraries to consider assuming responsibility of the GEOSET studio. After several rounds of conversations and negotiations, an agreement was reached for the libraries to manage GEOSET commencing the summer of 2017. In agreement with the provost's office, the libraries took on the studio's operations. As part of the agreement, the libraries also took on the existing GEOSET director, who had been a collaborator of Sir Harry Kroto for many years. The role was funded at 50 percent of a full-time position.

When GEOSET moved into Dirac in 2014, the studio was opened with much fanfare and Bill Nye as the guest of honor. The studio was set up in a former copy room, which was remodeled to create a control room, studio, equipment storage, and one staff office. Following the opening, the studio was managed by the GEOSET director, who was also assigned to the chemistry faculty on a part-time basis. A team of student workers staffed the daily operations of the studio and assisted with off-site shoots for lectures and presentations around the university. While nestled away in an inconspicuous area within Dirac, the studio was very busy working with numerous academic departments to record events around campus and allowing students and faculty to utilize the studio to showcase their research and scholarship beyond the walls of FSU.

Initial Steps

Taking on this new service in 2016 proved to be a challenge, as there was a steep learning curve associated with using the technology in the studio and incorporating the operations into the libraries. Although the studio had been in the libraries for several years, there was no significant communication between the libraries and GEOSET. The studio was operated and funded externally, and what took place in there often seemed a mystery. The libraries team had to learn everything from scratch. The dean of the libraries asked the associate dean for research and learning services, who had the science library in his portfolio, to assume the management of the studio. Thus, the GEOSET director started to report to the associate dean, who engaged the director of STEM libraries to help with establishing communications and to find opportunities for collaborations. After an initial evaluation, which quickly identified that the studio was too busy and could not effectively be managed with only one part-time director, it was determined that there were two staff members at the library with interest and abilities to support the operations of the studio. Both of them already had components of technology assistance as part of their portfolios, and the new responsibilities were folded into their job descriptions. In addition, training sessions were offered to all staff in Dirac to familiarize them with the equipment and what services were offered through the studio.

The library staff team had to learn how to use the equipment and assess the studio's inventory, much of which was outdated or broken. The team met regularly with the GEOSET director to get to know him and to learn as much as possible from him since he had been part of the original design of the studio and had acquired the very specialized equipment. Library administration discovered that the library staff members were exceptionally technologically savvy. Working together, the GEOSET director and library staff members were able to support existing projects while taking on new requests for studio use and documenting campus events. After only a few short months, however, the GEOSET director accepted a position at another university. This imposed an accelerated time line to ensure that as much knowledge as possible was transferred and documented about the operations of the studio before the director left. During this transition time, it was decided that the service model would remain the same. The libraries then had to develop a job description for the director and hire a replacement as a full-time employee of the libraries.

Training

One particular example highlights the need for innovation and collaboration with this project. The GEOSET director was recording interviews for the graduate school to produce highlight reels for students who attend FSU. In the process of recording these interviews, the library staff would get on-the-job training, shadowing the director and assisting him with the production of these videos. A training manual was created to document important information on the technology and resources of GEOSET, including links to YouTube tutorials about how to operate the cameras. Dirac staff were trained in the operation of the following programs and equipment: Camtasia, Mediasite Recorder, Black Magic 4K production camera, two Canon X300 cameras, and the Behringer Eurodesk sound mixer.

During the recordings, Camtasia and Mediasite were the software programs most often used. Camtasia is a software suite for editing video and audio. Mediasite is an integrated hardware and software solution that captures footage from multiple cameras and composes the footage into a template and live-streams the content. Ideally, staff would have had significant time to learn how to use these programs prior to being asked to record; however, due to time constraints, the team needed to be trained prior to the director leaving. Training by the outgoing GEOSET director was conducted during scheduled recording sessions, and staff were guided on how to capture recordings from the production cameras onto Mediasite. They were then taught how to perform basic edits of the captured footage using Camtasia.

It was eventually determined that, over time, the studio would be aligned with the extended campus and distance services librarian, who also reported to the associate dean for research and learning services. The Dirac staff who were trained in the operations of GEOSET continued to work on GEOSET; however, they now had dual reporting lines for their work. These staff members now had to coordinate with the extended campus librarian and the STEM libraries director to determine policies and bookings for the studio.

Prior to the original director leaving FSU, GEOSET maintained a staff of four to six student interns who were federal work study students, thus incurring no cost to the studio, which did not have an HR budget for student workers. The services that were provided at that time included video editing, equipment loaning, consultations, and recordings in-studio and off-site. The Dirac staff attempted to replicate these services, but due to lack of time and knowledge, requests for GEOSET were handled on a case-by-case basis and services were not actively advertised on the GEOSET's or library's website.

The process for booking the studio involved patrons going through a legacy website that had not yet been incorporated into the library's web infrastructure. FSU students and faculty could submit a request to schedule a consultation or recording session at the studio. The request included a brief project description, a general project time line with due dates, and contact information. Library staff reviewed the request and contacted the patrons to set up a consultation to determine specific project needs and to discuss how the libraries and GEOSET could help them achieve their goals. During the consultation, the staff would show the studio and equipment and gather information on patron expectations for the session. The consultations were structured to determine equipment needs, recording location, and whether video editing was required.

If staff members felt that there was too much of a time commitment or if the project was outside of their level of technical knowledge, they were empowered to turn down requests. In this scenario, staff would provide a referral to other video production services on campus or a list of commercial providers. It was important for the associate dean and the STEM libraries director to establish that the library staff managing the studio were empowered to decline or reroute requests if necessary. This is significant because establishing a level of service was a delicate process due to the amount of staffing time already directed toward existing projects involving GEOSET that predated the libraries' responsibility for the studio. Eventually, plans were made to create a new position to direct the studio and for the incoming director to have the space to create a new vision and direction for GEOSET in alignment with the libraries' mission and objectives.

Challenges and Opportunities

One of the largest challenges with running GEOSET during this period was staffing availability. When the previous director was working with the university, he had a staff of four to six student interns each semester. While the full Dirac staff was given training on how to operate in the studio, two staff were primarily responsible for coordinating the bookings. Both of these staff members worked the afternoon and closing shifts at Dirac, so availability for bookings was limited to their work schedules. Depending on the time and length of the booking sessions requested, staff would have to coordinate with their supervisor to adjust their own schedule or reroute the request to a different office on campus.

The additional workload for all who participated, but, in particular, for the two staff members involved, was significant. However, there was a high level of enthusiasm because everyone at the library was excited about the opportunity to learn and teach others how to create videos, podcasts, and other emerging forms of media. These assignments required flexibility since absorbing the additional responsibilities required renegotiating specific aspects of job descriptions so that they could spend the amount of time needed to manage the studio.

One strategy that was used to provide some temporary staffing stability was to recruit one of the library student workers to be an intern and help with recordings at GEOSET. The student was an information technology undergraduate student who received class credit for her time in the studio. While staffing was a challenge, this student was provided with a rewarding professional development opportunity that she described as the highlight of her three-year tenure with the libraries. Leveraging these opportunities was important to sustain the studio and the responsibilities inherited.

Learning how to actually operate the equipment within GEOSET proved to be a significant hurdle. Documentation left behind by the previous director was helpful but did not answer all the questions. For example, it did not include instructions on how to operate specific equipment, so a combination of trial and error, and using YouTube tutorials as backup, was the only way to advance many of the projects. When acquiring GEOSET, the Dirac staff found that there was no existing inventory list of the equipment in the studio, its condition, or who owned it. The studio had been inherited from the chemistry department, but, as was later discovered, equipment ownership had been poorly documented. Creating an inventory would be necessary before moving forward with training. Again, while this learning curve was a challenge, it provided an opportunity for library staff to stretch their skills beyond their current position and to gain skills to advance their careers. The skills associated with operating a multimedia studio, such as filming and video editing, are useful and highly marketable. Library staff appreciated the opportunity to operate the studio until a new director could be put in place.

Hiring a Director

Following the departure of the original director of GEOSET, the libraries had to hire a new director. In the time since the libraries were asked to take on the management of the studio, significant progress had been made regarding learning about the needs of library patrons and what it would take to manage the operations successfully. In addition, the libraries' administration had been in continued negotiations and conversations with the provost's office and other campus partners to determine a path forward. Now under the supervision of the distance and extended campus librarian, a new component was added to the job, which was to help her with managing the services to international programs. In designing this position, administration saw lots of synergies between the technology available in the recording studio and the need to produce video content for students and faculty abroad. The expanded responsibilities would be supported by a dedicated staff person reporting to the director of GEOSET. With the new position, staffing increased from one part-time director to a full-time director and a full-time staff person who both had significant portions of their time allocated to working on GEOSET. The position was advertised with the title of digital media and extended campus manager in May 2018. Response to the job advertisement was positive. An offer was made in June 2018. With the increased staffing, equipment in GEOSET was inventoried and updated, several projects for the libraries and campus partners were completed, and the GEOSET website was absorbed into the libraries' web infrastructure, which has allowed alignment of the GEOSET services with the libraries' reservation systems.

Next Steps

GEOSET remains in operation under the new director, who works with stakeholders in the library and across campus to develop and evolve the studio's vision. As the demand for the GEOSET services grows, associated staff members are working on developing a more refined service model and making sure that the operations of GEOSET are staffed properly to operate the studio and maintain the high quality of output.

ESTABLISHING A 3D PRINTING SERVICE

Unlike the previous initiative where the libraries acquired and assumed responsibility for the operation of an established multimedia production studio, this example highlights the implementation of a new 3D printing program and setting up the first 3D printer in the FSU libraries. Advantages of starting a new service from the ground up are that there are no inherited expectations and the program can grow at a rate congruent with existing staff. However, in as much as this is a new opportunity for the libraries, there were, as expected, several challenges to building this new service. Workflow issues, logistical challenges, and strategies for overcoming impediments will be discussed. Readers may find that much of the workflow detailed in this chapter and technology used can be adapted to other institutions.

The first 3D printer was purchased by the libraries' technology department in 2014 as a pilot to test the usability of the machine and to explore what kind of impact this technology could have for students and faculty in their research and scholarship. Many other libraries were exploring the idea of makerspaces, and the FSU libraries were equally interested in experimenting. One of the ways FSU libraries deploy new technology for student use is to purchase items to explore so that staff members can teach themselves how to use the technology before assisting users. A summer testing period allowed the IT associates to become familiar with the machine and software behind the scenes before making the service publicly available. At the end of the summer, the printer was moved to Dirac, where the librarians were asked to build a service model around the technology. The librarians were excited about the new technology and eager to explore the applications around the 3D printer for themselves.

The first printer purchased was a MakerBot Replicator 2. After some consultation, agreement was reached to place the printer in one of the science librarians' offices to observe it in order to develop a consultation model. In this first iteration, the librarian would meet with interested faculty and students to discuss their interests and needs related to 3D printing. Essentially, they would meet with her and discuss what they needed printed and she would print it for them. As demand for this service began to rise, the printer was being used regularly, which resulted in a need to move it out of an office. For greater visibility, it was moved next to the café area on the main floor of Dirac. Placing the printer within patrons' view sparked interest, and the number of requests continued to rise. In the first full year that the library offered 3D printing, there were over four hundred requests printed for faculty and students. By 2016, the printer failed and had to be replaced. However, given the success of the program, the libraries purchased two 3D printers. One replaced the original printer in Dirac, and a second one was placed in the technology area in the main library.

Establishing a Workflow

With the rapidly escalating demand for 3D printing, the libraries had to establish a workflow that allowed for the 3D printer to run during most of the library's opening hours. This proved to be challenging but was instrumental in meeting the needs of our scholars as well as making the service visible. The need to establish a workflow was important, and the process that evolved over approximately two years is described below.

The first step in the printing process is the submission of a design via an online form located on the libraries' website. In addition, a link to this form was also provided in the digital signage in the libraries as well as on the table where the 3D printer was located. Students were encouraged to submit requests if the printers grabbed their attention. The following items were required on the form: first and last name, email address, status (undergraduate student, graduate student, faculty, staff, or other), what the model is intended for (class assignment, research project, teaching, personal, or other), a zip file of the print request in .stl format with the naming convention of FSUID_Month_Day_Year.stl, preferred color, date required, short description of the print, and consent to pictures being taken of their print to share on the 3D printing website.

Additional optional information was requested, such as desired dimensions for the product (length, height, and width in millimeters) and any additional notes they wished to share. All of this information allowed staff to prioritize the printing. Printing was free and, while a lot of latitude was allowed, priority was given to requests intended for educational use.

Tracking Submissions

To keep track of submissions, the staff used a shared Google spreadsheet to record the details of all the prints run on the 3D printers. This sheet is populated with information provided by the print request form. To supplement the information, staff add details such as date of entry, printing status, color, print dimensions, amount of filament used, and estimated print time. This information informs the growth and development of the 3D printing program and serves as a knowledge base of specifics regarding all the print jobs that have been conducted at Dirac.

The progress of the print requests is tracked by the print status found in the Google spreadsheet. The first stage of the process is "Under Review." Each print request is inspected to make sure the requested print does not break any of the policies set forth by the library or is not in violation of any known copyright. The person doing the review also verifies that the print size does not exceed the physical constraints of the printer. If the request breaks the library's printing policies, the printing status is changed to "Canceled" and an email is sent to the patron explaining why his or her printing request was not sent to print. If staff see a problem in the design, such as being too big or too small for the printer's capabilities, the status is changed to "Revisions Needed" and a staff member will reach out to the patron to explain that the design needs to be revised. The requester is offered a chance to arrange a face-to-face consultation to talk about the required changes. If a face-to-face consultation is declined, the staff will supply a few suggested edits to maximize the success of the print. If the patron chooses not to take either of these options, the printing status is changed to "Declined" and the print is canceled.

Printing Submissions

Once any necessary edits are made, the file is loaded into Cura (a 3D print management tool), where the staff scales the design to the correct dimensions, adds support structures needed to ensure a successful print, and sets the infill setting (density of the object). Staff record the estimated printing time and the amount of filament used in the Google spreadsheet. Once this information is recorded, the "G-code" is exported and the printing status in the Google spreadsheet is changed to "G-Code Ready." G-code is essentially human-created language that tells the 3D printer how to print the object and contains command lines that tell the printer how to move. The G-code file is loaded into a shared Google file and placed into either the high-priority or low-priority file. Through this process, a large number of requests can be processed at one time, with all the G-codes available to all library staff, regardless of shift.

The next step in the workflow is to set up the printing queue. Every day, the G-codes are organized based on priority, print time, and color of filament, and two or three of the prints are uploaded to the Octoprint queue for each of the LulzBot printers. The LulzBots were purchased in 2016 to replace the original MakerBot printer. The printing status is then changed to "Queued for Printing," which enables the day or night staff to quickly start prints during busy times of the day and helps staff stay on top of the amount of submissions coming into the library. When a print is started, the status is changed to "Currently Printing."

While the item is printing, the library staff is able to monitor the progress of the print via small webcams set up by the printing bed. This allows the staff to be at their personal desks tending to other duties and to periodically check the printer to make sure nothing has gone wrong after starting the print. If the print is finished, the status in the spreadsheet is changed to "Print Complete" and an email is sent to the patron notifying him or her that the print is ready for pickup at the circulation desk. If a problem occurs during the printing process and the staff member on duty is unable to troubleshoot the problem, be it a hardware issue or a problem in the design, the print is stopped and the status is changed to "Incomplete." When this happens, the library staff who support software and technology services attempt more advanced troubleshooting, and if needed the library IT team is called in for further assistance. Once the problem is fixed, the print is reattempted and the status is once again changed to "Currently Printing."

When the email about the completed print is sent, the requester is asked to come to the Dirac Science Library Circulation Desk to pick it up. A valid FSU ID must be presented to confirm the patron's name, and a basic pickup form must be signed. This form contains a line for the number of pieces associated with the print, the name of the print, the date the print was completed, and the printed name of the patron who is to pick up the print. The form must be signed and dated before a patron is allowed to take the print. The signed pickup sheets are kept for reference in case questions arise later regarding the pickup of the print. Finally, the print status in the Google spreadsheet is changed to "Picked Up."

Policies

One particular and important challenge was determining the policies under which the program would operate. Not wanting to reinvent the wheel and to expedite the implementation of the service, staff reviewed current 3D printing policies from other academic institutions. This led to the creation of policies such as no printing of weapons or pieces that could be assembled into weapons and no creating drug paraphernalia. While the survey of other institutional policies helped provide some guidance, staff still had to answer questions such as the following:

- Would prints for personal use be allowed? If so, how many personal use prints could a single patron request during a semester?

- Could patrons ask to print objects that could be considered to be under copyright, such as Dungeons and Dragons figurines?
- How large of a print job could we allow?

The 3D printers were purchased with assistance from student technology fees, which meant that library staff were determined to ensure that students had as much access to the 3D printers as possible. The service was overwhelmingly used by students and managing staff, and faculty requests did not take much time or effort. Since student technology fees are funded from tuition, there needed to be enough time on the printer for students to use the printers for research and learning purposes. This was initially resolved by prioritizing academic print requests above experimental or hobby requests. For experimental prints, initially there was no restriction unless the model was a weapon, which was prohibited. The original funding for the printer enabled a substantial amount of filament to be purchased. Near the end of 2017, the filament supply ran out due to the popularity of the service. Using the data collected, staff examined the use of the printer and decided to limit the amount of filament that could be used for a recreational request in order to avoid running short on filament supplies again. The cap was set at one hundred grams per print. Setting this limit was important since it allowed the libraries to maintain 3D printing as a free service to students and faculty.

Updating and Expanding Equipment

Over time, the original MakerBot printer experienced several malfunctions, and it became more sensible to purchase a new printer. Since the first device printed almost one thousand items in just over two years, it was decided that two printers should be purchased. The two printers purchased were Lulzbot Taz 6s and included several rolls of filament. Making these two new printers ready to be put into service required overcoming a few technical hurdles. The first was the need to change out the stock of filament from 1.75-mm polyactic acid (PLA) filament to a larger 3.00-mm ColorFabb nGen and a limited stock of 3.00-mm acrylonitrile butadiene styrene (ABS) filament.

The change in filament size and type was required to meet the specifications of the filament extruder of the LulzBot printers. Library staff also spent some time comparing the different brands of PLA filament to determine which brand would be most cost-effective. The original filament used with the MakerBot printer, PLA, worked with the original printer because it did not require a heated bed, something the MakerBot did not have. It is also a firm printing material that tended to have few warping issues, which means that print jobs came out looking normal rather than deformed or warped. The replacement filament chosen for use with the LulzBot printer was also a PLA but came from a brand called ColorFabb nGen. This filament shares properties of the original PLA filament in that it is a stiff but brittle printing material. This filament has a higher heat resistance, making it a compatible filament for printers with a heated bed platform. The nGen filament also came in a variety of colors that the staff were eager to experiment with. It also enabled patrons to select from a limited number of colors for their prints.

The two PLA filaments discussed previously were used for the majority of the print requests submitted by students and faculty. However, there was one research project being conducted at FSU's Center for Advanced Power Systems that required printing prototype designs of cable insulators for electrical conductivity tests. To test these prototypes, a special filament was requested that could withstand higher temperatures than the PLA, leading to the use of the ABS filament. This example highlights the fact that, while things like filament types for most types of projects can be standardized, there still needs to be room for flexibility for special projects.

When upgrading printers, computer connections that run the printers and monitors needed to be completely reconfigured. The MakerBot was restricted to a direct desktop computer connection, which required the libraries to have a dedicated computer that was used solely to run the printer connected to it. With the newer LulzBot printers, a cloud-based printer was set up through a system called OctoPrint. OctoPrint allowed the 3D printing team to run and monitor their printers from a password-protected website, giving them freedom to work from any computer connected to the library's network. In addition to using a cloud program to manage the prints, an open-source software called Cura was used to design and edit the 3D print requests, which meant that library staff could lean on the open-source community to troubleshoot issues.

Other Challenges

Library staff learned to deal with the occasional hardware malfunction. The original MakerBot printer had a number of issues that required troubleshooting. Filament reels would get stuck in knots, causing the print to fail. The extruder was prone to getting clogged with broken filament and, due to the assembly of the printer, required the extruder to be completely disassembled to address the clog. The MakerBot was also prone to freezing in the middle of prints, which occurred randomly. There were often a number of solutions for these issues, including the MakerBot requiring a firmware update, addressing a clog inside of the extruder, or determining that it was a faulty model. One day, the MakerBot powered down on its own, and upon closer inspection, it turned out that the motherboard was no longer working. This prompted the purchase of replacement printers.

One frequently occurring problem encountered when the library first acquired the LulzBot printers was the clogging of the extruder head on the printer. This would happen for two different reasons. First, some filament would get stuck on the outside of the extruder, thereby blocking any other filament from getting out, subsequently burning the filament that touched the outside of the extruder head. Second, sometimes the extruder head would become clogged from the inside due to the filament feeder pushing too much filament into the feeder before it was appropriately melted, thus getting the filament jammed into the extruder. These problems would require stopping the printer and cleaning the extruder head, then slowly reintroducing filament back into the extruder and running several millimeters through the extruder to ensure it had no clogs. On rare occasions, students asked to print with acrylonitrile butadiene styrene (ABS) filament. Since ABS is amorphous, it has no true melting point, so it requires a lot of trial and error in order to successfully print with it.

While a workflow has been established that allows the day and night shifts at the library to keep the 3D printers running nearly 24/7, there have been issues of maintaining consistent levels of service due to changes in library staff. First, the service was set up as a managed service by the librarians. However, after some turnover in the librarian ranks and with the increasing popularity of the service, the workload was no longer manageable by librarians. Thus the management of the service was assigned to two members of the staff who work the overnight shift. This means they have more time to troubleshoot design and hardware problems. They also possessed knowledge of technology that helped support students' needs. The staff members created a basic training session for the day-shift staff and librarians covering basic hardware troubleshooting, how to prepare the printer for a print, how to start the print, and the process for removal of the object. The day shift was then able to keep the printers running during the day and keep prints in the queue to a manageable list.

When someone leaves his or her position, the concern is that all of that person's experience is difficult to document, and the replacement has to be trained to use the printers, a function that is usually not a formal part of the position description. As a result, the queue can become backed up with requests, and if a problem occurs during a running print job, newer staff may not know how to troubleshoot the problem.

Opportunities

Originally, the 3D program was intended for students to gain exposure and access to an emerging area of technology, and the volume and high number of individual student users are evidence of the libraries having succeeded. Each year, anywhere from three hundred to five hundred items are printed for faculty and students. While the libraries encouraged the use of the printers for personal and "fun" projects, approximately half of the submissions are for classroom use or research. For example, one of FSU's research centers, the Center for Advanced Power Systems, sent some of their student researchers to the library to work with staff to print a prototype with special filament that was used to test electrical conductivity. Within a few days, these student researchers were able to learn how to edit their model so that it would be printable. On several occasions, students from the engineering school utilized the printers to help with their senior design projects, also known as a large group capstone project, that happens every fall semester. These specific examples are exactly why the library wanted to provide 3D printers for exploratory use in the first place.

Developing the 3D program provided professional development opportunities for staff at Dirac, similar to the previous example of operating the GEOSET studio. Staff developed project management and critical thinking skills as they were largely responsible for coordinating workflows and operations of the program. In addition to learning how to operate the printers, library staff also learned how to draw and edit 3D models in free CAD software such as TinkerCAD. This enhanced the service model because they were now able to help patrons fix their models and to modify requests.

Next Steps

Many other academic units at FSU now have 3D printers, and there is a new facility, called the Hub, which has over thirty 3D printers that can be used by the FSU community. While patrons are still utilizing the printers in the library, our organization is considering new ways to leverage this technology to help with information literacy initiatives within the library. Librarians at FSU have been discussing ways to incorporate 3D printing technologies into existing information literacy initiatives. There are opportunities for the libraries to teach 3D modeling software, such as TinkerCAD, which could be incorporated into the GIS and statistical software workshop offerings. While there are plans to continue offering 3D printing services to patrons, the libraries are actively seeking ways to expand into services that further strengthen students' information literacy and critical thinking skills.

CONCLUSION

To stay at the forefront of working with scholars, the libraries must grow in a way that meets the evolving needs of its campus by showing leadership in technology and knowledge acquisition. It is necessary to be bold in developing programs and services and trust in staff members' ability to learn and to facilitate a structure that is nimble and responsive to students' ever-changing needs.

The examples of the 3D printing service and a library-managed multimedia studio are two initiatives that have advanced FSU libraries by enhancing teaching and learning activities for students and faculty. In both instances, there was an iterative approach to maintaining and developing these services. Even though one service was designed from scratch and the other was "inherited," the authors found that, in both cases, they and their staff had to learn quickly how to operate and scale the technologies. When they encountered challenges, they discovered that they had the creativity and ability to adjust and overcome the challenges. This not only allowed for flexibility in the way services are provided but also allowed the library organization to meet demands without being delayed by significant front-end planning.

While these two initiatives are examples of providing new services with limited time and resources, they also highlight the incorporation of two of the organization's values: empowerment and innovation. In order to foster a spirit of innovation in the organization, it is important to cultivate an environment that welcomes experimentation with new and different ideas, methods, and processes. In an effort to encourage the development of new ideas, it is necessary to acknowledge and accept that things may go in unexpected directions and that failure is often part of the process of innovation. Specifically, the 3D printing program highlights how staff experimented with new processes and procedures in order to provide a new service for the campus. As technology broke and problems were encountered, library staff used these challenges as learning opportunities to inform the next iteration of service.

To foster a culture of empowerment, individuals at all levels of the organization must be equipped and trained to step in to handle situations as they arise. Much of the work of transitioning GEOSET into the purview of the libraries and creating a new 3D printing service happened at the same time and with the same staff at the Dirac Science Library. Their efforts were instrumental in the success of both programs. This required flexibility in assuming new responsibilities and expanding previous position descriptions. As a result, an environment was created where library staff were empowered to create and test new versions of the 3D printing service model and worked with campus partners to push their own technical expertise.

Throughout these two experiences, there was a collaborative tone that prioritized information sharing and cross training so that as many people as possible could step in as needed to help with either printing or managing the studio. Cross training allowed for the 3D printers to be in operation at all times that the Dirac Science Library was open. Information sharing and collaboration allowed for daytime staff to field consultations for GEOSET use that would be conducted by nighttime staff. While this was key in the programs' initial success, every time somebody left the organization, library staff struggled to not only compensate for the lack of contribution from the empty staff position but also to cope with the loss of knowledge and expertise that also left with the person. This highlights the importance of documentation and creating organizational knowledge banks where leaders can gain a glimpse of "who knows what" and proactively create structures for information sharing and cross training.

Index

Applied Engineering and Technology (AET) Library, 13, 15, 16
Agisoft Photoscan, 40, 42
ArcGIS, 15, 28
Arduino, 51, 53, 65
augmented reality (AR), xiii, xiv, 1, 3, 4, 9, 14, 21, 22, 37, 38, 46

caliper, 51, 56, 62
Center for Instructional Technology and Training (CITT), 9

GatorVR, 6
GroupSpot, 14, 16, 17, 18, 20, 21, 22

HoloLens, xiii, xiv, 2, 3, 4, 5, 37, 38, 39, 41, 42, 43, 44, 45, 46, 47, 48
holograms, 37, 38, 40, 42, 43, 44, 45, 46, 47, 48
HTC Vive, xiii, 2, 5, 6, 8, 9, 10, 54

lightboard, xiv, 25, 31, 32, 33, 34, 35

Made@UF, 3, 4, 5, 6, 8, 9
makerspaces, xi, xii, xiii, 52, 53, 67, 85
mixed reality, 2, 3, 4

NetSupport, 17, 18

Oculus, xiii, 2, 3, 4, 6, 8, 9, 10, 54, 56

Photoscan, 42, 43
Pix4D, 41

Queerskins: A Love Story, 8

Solstice, xiv, 25, 30

TeamSpot, 17, 22
Thingiverse, 47
TightVNC, 17, 18, 21

Unimersiv, 8
Unity 3D, xiii, 3, 4, 8, 9, 44, 45, 46, 47
Unreal, 3, 4

Valve, 2
virtual reality (VR), xii, xiii, xiv, 1, 2, 3, 4, 5, 6, 8, 9, 10, 11, 21, 22, 37, 38, 51, 53, 54, 56

whiteboard, 17, 19, 21, 53, 54
workstations, xii, 15, 17, 18, 22, 28

About the Editor and Contributors

Beth Thomsett-Scott has been serving as the head of the Engineering Library at the Pennsylvania State University (Penn State) since March 2017. She is the liaison to the College of Engineering and consults with faculty, staff, and students to ensure their needs are met through services, instructing, and collections. Beth holds a BSc, MSc, and MLIS. She has published in a variety of journals and presented conference sessions in the areas of user services, mentoring and training reference staff and students, and technology. Her passions include virtual reference, website usability, user satisfaction studies, and technologies for reference, instruction, and liaison.

* * *

Becca Greenstein (she/her/hers) is the STEM librarian at Northwestern University Libraries, where she serves as liaison to mathematics, statistics, biological sciences, and biomedical engineering. She is excited to have had the opportunity to gather statistics about the use of technology in the renovated Mudd Library and hopes that patrons will continue to use the services available to them. She is interested in open access, creating inclusive library environments, research metrics, and information access for everyone: users and nonusers alike.

Kelly Grove has been a STEM research and learning librarian at Florida State University since 2017. She has developed a strong research interest in areas of STEM information literacy, the cost of doing research, Open Educational Resources, and subject librarianship. She is a current member of American Library Association, Association of College and Research Libraries, Florida Library Association, and the American Society of Engineering Education.

Matt Hayward is the STEM librarian at the University of Texas at San Antonio. He has worked in this capacity for two years and has a background in chemistry and clinical psychology. His research interests include instructional technology, experiential learning, and open data and research data management.

Christie Hurrell is the digital initiatives and scholarly communications librarian at the University of Calgary. Her role involves advancing digital research initiatives and partnerships, working on open access and scholarly communication initiatives, and coordinating Lab NEXT, the library's digital scholarship collaboration space and makerspace. Christie's research and practice interests stem from her interest in new ways of sharing and tracking the impact of research.

Renaine Julian is the director of STEM Libraries at Florida State University. In this role, he oversees a team of science librarians and staff that provide support for STEM scholars across the research and learning life cycles. Prior to that, Renaine served at Florida State University as a data research librarian, STEM data and research librarian, as well as the associate director for STEM Libraries. Renaine has an MLIS, an MS in urban and regional planning, and a BS in political science all from Florida State University. His research interests include library leadership and administration, scholarly communication, and open science.

Joshua Julien was the STEM data and software supervisor at the Dirac Science Library when the chapter was written. He is now a Librarian I trainee at the Deltona Regional Library and is working on his MLIS from Florida State University. Joshua is well versed in 3D principles and practice and related technology.

Kari Kozak is the head of the Lichtenberger Engineering Library at The University of Iowa. She provides instruction, reference, and consultation services to students, faculty, and staff within the departments and research centers in the College of Engineering as well as the Department of Computer Science. Kari holds bachelor's degrees in meteorology and environmental studies from Iowa State and a master's degree in library science from the University of North Carolina–Chapel Hill. Kari's areas of interest include outreach, instruction, innovation, and design.

Paul McMonigle is the engineering instruction librarian at Penn State University. He is involved in outreach and student engagement programs geared toward faculty and students in the university's College of Engineering. His research interests include incorporating technology into information literacy courses for engineering students, the creation and assessment of outreach programs for STEM students, and discovering innovative ways to attract more military veteran students into engineering majors.

Michael Meth serves as associate dean for research and learning services for Florida State University (FSU) Libraries, where he manages a team dedicated to shaping the libraries' services for students and faculty, creating programs and partnerships that enhance and support research at all levels, and ensuring that the libraries are integrated into teaching and learning at FSU. Before coming to FSU, Michael was a librarian at the University of Toronto (UofT) libraries. He holds a master of information studies from UofT's Faculty of Information Studies (now the iSchool) and a bachelor of business administration from the Schulich School of Business at York University.

Samuel Putnam is the engineering education librarian and director of MADE@UF, an extended reality development space, at Marston Science Library at the University of Florida. His research focuses on innovative and multimodal instruction practices as a means to promote information literacy. In this work, Putnam engages with extended reality as a tool in teaching and learning as well as an avenue for information creation, and he critically examines XR and its role in the current information ecosystem.

Marc Stoeckle is the research and learning librarian for the School of Creative and Performing Arts and the School of Languages, Linguistics, Literatures, and Cultures at the University of Calgary. He is passionate about new technology as learning resources, and his current research focuses on finding better ways to connect digital and analog resources to make them more easily accessible for research, learning, and teaching.

Dean Walton is the Lorry I. Lokey Science and Technology Outreach Librarian at the University of Oregon. His research interests are in the use of new tools to collect, curate, and display scientific information. As a past ecologist, he continues to focus on the exploration and collection of data in this field. He particularly works on issues relating to mapping, geographic information systems, and remotely sensed data.

www.ingramcontent.com/pod-product-compliance
Lightning Source LLC
Chambersburg PA
CBHW031554300426
44111CB00006BA/310